DEMOCRACY
AND THE INDIVIDUAL

by
CARLETON KEMP ALLEN
Warden of Rhodes House, Oxford

OXFORD UNIVERSITY PRESS
LONDON   NEW YORK   TORONTO

First published 1943
Second impression (reset) 1945

PRINTED IN GREAT BRITAIN
645.6306

CONTENTS

CONTENTS

INTRODUCTORY

OUR cause in the present war suffers from the handicap that, although we are all certain that we are fighting to maintain democracy, many of us are not clear in our minds about the nature of the thing for which we are fighting. Ask any six intelligent men what they understand by democracy and there will be six answers so different that there seems to be hardly any common basis at all.

... Streit tells us that democracy is government of the totality by the majority for the sake equally of each minority of one'; these descriptions leave a great many troublesome questions unanswered. Most writers, indeed, agree that democracy is incapable of accurate definition. We must look for its meaning in something other than a formula, for all formulas are good servants but bad masters; but if we cannot be precise about the letter, we must at least try to be clear about the spirit.

Again, it is evident that among modern democracies there are such profound differences not only of detail but of principle that it is difficult to disengage ele-

[1] *Modern Democracies*, I viii, and cf. I 25-26.
[2] *Union Now*, 22.

ments common to them all. To take three examples, Great Britain, the United States, and France exhibit enormous variations in their whole political and governmental structure, and, in some respects, in their whole social outlook. There are many people in America who find it difficult to believe that England, with its monarchy and its House of Lords and its supposed 'ruling class', is a democracy at all. They would certainly be startled by the suggestion—which I, for one, should be prepared to make—that the British Empire is the largest and most remarkable democratic institution in the world, or in history. It is one of the underlying weaknesses in Mr. Streit's proposal for Federal Union that he assumes that because different states have *some* democratic elements in common, they will necessarily coalesce into a single form of government. States may be 'democratic' in their own several ways, and yet may be unassimilable, or at least highly incompatible, in the actual processes of government. When he specifies the proposed members of his federation, Mr. Streit feels bound to exclude Russia, because, being based on a one-party system, it cannot be considered democratic. Most of us would agree in that opinion, and indeed I imagine that most Russians would assent to it. Some Russians, however, might say that since 1936 Russia has had a constitution which, in form at least, comprises most of the ordinary 'democratic' arrangements, and that she has gone much farther towards true democracy (according to one interpretation of it) than any other modern country by having established a real or supposed 'classless society'.

Amid these many variations of fact and theory, it is not surprising to find the most recent exponent of

'The Modern Democratic State', Mr. A. D. Lindsay, complaining that 'indecisive woolliness is the curse of much modern democratic thought.' Perhaps in this respect we are not, in reality, worse off than our enemies, for their theories of the omnipotent State or Race resolve themselves, on analysis, into 'woolliness' of the most tangled kind—the more delusive because it reacts against the 'indecisiveness' of democratic doctrine by an artificial decisiveness which ends in nothing but bombast. 'Honest doubt' about democratic forms and methods is itself a democratic frame of mind, and is infinitely healthier than the fanatical positiveness of New Orders, New Roman Empires, and such sounding brass as *Reich*, *Raum und Rasse* or *Blut und Erde*. Nevertheless, there is a point beyond which 'honest doubt' may become catalepsy of mind and will and conviction, or may degenerate into the mere thoughtless repetition of catchwords and slogans —a formidable enemy of intelligent policy in all democratic communities.

Woolliness of thinking, however, is not the same thing as conviction about a 'way of life' which is none the less spiritually deep-seated and practically operative because the ordinary man would find it difficult to formulate in apt and comprehensive words. Mr. Walter Lippmann[1] has written of 'mystical' and 'literal' democracy—the one an indefinable faith that 'the personality of every man and woman is sacred and inviolable', the other a belief that good government and political wisdom are to be found by counting noses. Counting of noses may be demonstrably absurd, and even counting of souls, like every act of faith, leaves the sceptic unanswered. The great prac-

[1] Cited Lindsay, *The Modern Democratic State*, p. 254.

tical problem of democracy is to reconcile the business of nose-counting, some measure of which is indispensable to the majoritarian principle, with the 'mystical' element on which alone, in the last analysis, rests our respect and solicitude for the human individual as such.

To-day, fighting not only for our 'way of life', but for life itself, we take our faith so much for granted that we forget how new it is in the world. Little more than a century ago, though the great experiment had been made in the New World, there was only one democracy in Europe, and that weak and diminutive —Switzerland. England could claim to be democratic in so far as she had established, at the cost of two revolutions, the principle of Parliamentary rule and constitutional monarchy; but her Parliament was, according to modern notions, preposterously unrepresentative, and William Pitt himself sat for a constituency which became a byword for the rottenness of boroughs. The democracies of the ancient world had been parentheses in history. It is a commonplace to say that the city-democracy of Athens, tiny, short-lived, always insecure, and economically based, in large measure, on slave labour, offers no analogy to any modern State. As for Rome, it is open to question whether its Republic was ever a democracy at all; it always hovered on the edge of dictatorship and passed almost inevitably into deified monarchy. It is true that the imperial office retained for some three centuries the fiction of popular sanction and some reality of constitutionalism in the powers of the senate; but eventually it became an open military dictatorship and gave to the world the maxim *princeps legibus solutus est*—the watchword of all subsequent

European Caesarism (though never in England).

Even if ancient democratic systems can be said to have had much influence upon later political systems, little of that influence remained, in actual social institutions, in the eighteenth century. The feudal structure and the unity of Christendom had long since given place to the new nationalism which was embodied in the idea of territorial sovereignty. The prevailing view of history and of established institutions was fatalistic, or, at the least, passive; what had to be, was, and what was, had to be; good or ill, it was part of the preordained scheme of things, and human contrivance could do little to change it. So far as men speculated upon a better state of society, they looked backward to a Paradise Lost, or a Golden Age, but seldom forward to a better world for a better mankind; for that had been lost for ever by the Fall from Grace, it was to be regained only in heaven, and the mere thought of it on earth was not only futile but impious. These fantasies of the past were a sort of imaginary compensation for the *vis inertiae* of resigned acquiescence and mental indolence. 'It is indisputable,' wrote Maine of the Old Order, 'that much the greatest part of mankind has never shown a particle of desire that its civil institutions should be improved since the moment when external completeness was first given to them by their embodiment in some permanent record.' Thus the political mood was static; and the very word reminds us that the situation of the individual in society was governed by the notion of status. 'The movement of progressive societies,' in Maine's famous phrase, had not yet made it possible for the individual to determine, by his own efforts, his rung upon the social ladder. Government rested upon the supreme principle of authority. In France, Bodin had carried *majestas* to its highest point of absolutism; in England, Hobbes had proclaimed the natural depravity of man and his need of authority to save him from instinctive lawlessness; and Hobbes's corollary was the unlimited sovereignty of authority, once it had been established by an imaginary compact, and the divorce of law from morality. But in England also, it is true, absolutism had brought a king to the scaffold, and brother had slain brother over the Divine Right; in England, too, after a second but bloodless revolution, John Locke had placed upon sovereignty the 'contractual' restraint of the consent of the governed. From the time of Bracton onwards, the Byzantine purple was never admitted to the British throne, and the ranks of the people, in some strange manner 'represented' at Westminster by an unrepresentative assembly, never sank to the status of the *sansculottes* of France. None the less, acceptance of the established order and of 'that station in life', submission to constituted authority, resignation to an imperfect society, and resolve, not to make it better, but at most to prevent it from becoming worse—these made the temper of good citizenship. Even in the early nineteenth century, when John Austin, first among Englishmen to do so, analysed the nature of law, he found its essence in 'determinate' authority and in command and obedience. Over all was a supreme Law of Nature, which could be invoked by the doctrinaire to lend to any dogma the majesty of revealed truth.

It was upon some such Old Order of thinking as this that Rousseauism burst. His equalitarianism and General Will were 'like a fire-bell in the night' (as

Thomas Jefferson wrote of the slavery issue in 1819)
and it clanged throughout the Western world. Lord
Acton was of opinion that Rousseau had 'produced
more effect with his pen' than any man who ever
lived. This was a New Order indeed! What it meant
to the idealists who had long dreamed of it can best
be studied in the poetry of Shelley. When he wrote
that 'the world's great age begins anew', he was
thinking not only of his beloved and romanticized
Hellas, which had thrown off her yoke of servitude,
but of a whole new 'world order'. The last words of
the poem express the aspirations of a lifetime:

> The world is weary of the past——
> Oh, might it die or rest at last!

The measure of disillusionment, which men like Burke
had always foreseen, was the measure of extravagant
hope, and it followed almost immediately upon the
first act of 'liberation'. Byron was a libertarian no less
ardent than Shelley, but while Shelley was hailing
the millennium he wrote:

> But France got drunk with blood to vomit crime,
> And fatal have her Saturnalia been
> To Freedom's cause, in every age and clime;
> Because the deadly days which we have seen,
> And vile ambition, that built up between
> Man and his hopes an adamantine wall,
> And the base pageant last upon the scene,
>   Are grown the pretext for the eternal thrall
>   Which nips life's tree, and dooms man's worst
>   —his second fall.

Nevertheless, the Utopians continued to believe that

the Revolution marked a wholly new epoch in human affairs. One finds this ingenuous faith in many unexpected places, long after the first enthusiastic acclaim of the New Order had been tempered by France's—and Europe's—subsequent distresses. That now neglected book, Mark Twain's *Life on the Mississippi* was published in 1874. In one of its chapters, the censorious Yankee element in Mark Twain criticizes indolent and unprogressive Southerners for being too much addicted to the romances of Sir Walter Scott. This literary vice is calculated to undo all the good work of the Democratic Age!

'Against the crimes of the French Revolution and of Bonaparte may be set two compensating benefactions: the Revolution broke the chains of the *ancien régime* and of the Church, and made a nation of abject slaves a nation of freemen; and Bonaparte instituted the setting of merit above birth, and also so completely stripped the divinity from royalty that, whereas crowned heads in Europe were gods before, they are only men since, and can never be gods again, but only figure-heads, and answerable for their acts like common clay. . . . Then comes Sir Walter Scott with his enchantments, and by his single might checks the wave of progress, and even turns it back; sets the world in love with dreams and phantoms; with decayed and swinish forms of religion; with decayed and degraded systems of government; with the sillinesses and emptinesses, sham grandeurs, sham gauds, and sham chivalries of a brainless and worthless long-vanished society. He did measureless harm; more real and lasting harm, perhaps, than any other individual that ever wrote.'

Poor Sir Walter! To think that his innocent

romances should be political poison capable of 'measureless harm'! Yet to this earnest, if unimaginative, critic, human history had begun in 1789 and all that had gone before was not only unimportant, but simply not to be thought of by men of goodwill. The same writer could see nothing in King Arthur and his Round Table except a subject for scornful satire. For him, all the brave who had lived before Agamemnon were better dead and better forgotten.

Absurd though this seems, it was probably an average 'sound' American view nearly a hundred years after the Revolution. It is needless to recall how the Declaration of Independence borrowed the very words of Rousseau to challenge the Old Order, and how his doctrines were translated into action in the most remarkable piece of 'social planning' which the world has ever seen. Here was the triumphant answer to the determinist view of history; an unprecedented political structure was devised and set in motion by men sitting round a table, and it has stood all strains (one almost fatal) for nearly a century and a half. Perhaps it is a personal bias which leads me to say that it was for the most part the work of lawyers, who are supposed to play such an unconstructive part in the community. If men had only remembered, it was not the first time in history that this feat of calculated contrivance in politics had been performed, for Athenian democracy itself was largely the work of one man, Cleisthenes.

It is also unnecessary, for present purposes, to relate how the New Order spread throughout Europe in the succeeding century. The causes were many, but, as Mr. Lindsay has observed, the prime impulses were two—in the idealistic sphere, Rousseauism and all the gospel of the Rights of Man; and in the material sphere, the Industrial Revolution. After a life brief indeed by comparison with the systems which preceded it, it is now assailed by a large section of humanity as mischievous in practice and false in theory. The supreme issue for us to-day is whether the Democratic Century is to be only another parenthesis in the history of government, or whether it will prove to be an infant which is now passing through one of the maladies of childhood and which, by developing its resistance to the germs of disease, will be the stronger and healthier in maturity. Democracy will have failed if it *merely* survives this war; it must emerge better and saner than it was before, or it will only stagger on to another and perhaps more formidable crisis. For that reason it is necessary to be clear in our minds that we fight, not merely to preserve, but to enlarge and to ameliorate.

Amid all the different interpretations of democracy and of what Mr. Lindsay calls its 'operative ideals', we can, I think, distinguish certain characteristics which are essential to its conception and to its working. In stating them, I am painfully aware that I shall be perpetuating commonplaces; but it is sometimes salutary to review our daily platitudes in order to discover, if we can, what we really mean by them, instead of repeating them by sheer force of habit without pausing to inquire whether they mean anything at all.

POLITICAL EQUALITY

The 'literal' equality of men, in mind, body, and attainments, is so manifestly contrary to experience and observation that nobody nowadays would seriously maintain it as the foundation of democratic faith.

Aristotle regarded it as the most fatal of fallacies, certain to deliver democracy into the hands of oligarchy or tyranny. Biologically, men are, always have been, and probably always will be, profoundly unequal; and no society can ever hope to be so composed that every citizen makes as valuable a contribution to its corporate life as every other. The 'mystical' equality of men is a wholly different conception. It means that every citizen, of whatever capacity, is entitled to what a German jurist calls 'consideration' (*Achten*) from all other members of society. Strong or weak, effective or non-effective, he is to be regarded as deserving such opportunities of self-development as he is capable of grasping, or even sheer protection and subsistence if he is incapable, through natural defects or undeserved misfortunes, of maintaining any foothold for himself in society. This view, that the human being, merely because he is such, possesses a quality which is worth safeguarding for its own sake is clearly a matter of faith, or hope, or charity, or all three. It cannot be justified on grounds of materialistic logic or expediency. If we were to govern society on purely biological principles, we should destroy or sterilize all our defectives and recalcitrants—as some, indeed, would have us do. Except in the case of the most heinous offenders, who have themselves violated the sanctity of individuality and of whom it is necessary to make the extreme example, democratic instinct utterly revolts from any such drastic physiological decimation. Indeed, this instinct is so strong that we still hesitate to take from the victim of incurable illness and merciless pain his last spark of life. Our 'respect for human life' is not based on horror or alarm at the physical extinction of an organism; the tragedies of accident

B

and disease, grim though they are, we must accept, for life would be intolerable if we were for ever mourning them; indeed, we seem to regard with singular equanimity the deplorable wastage of life every day upon our highways. The life which we respect is not merely the activating force of an animate biped; it is the quintessence of an individual creature.

In terms of religion it is the integument of a soul; and this starting-point of democracy is doubtless religious in origin. I suppose there has never been a time in the history of Christianity when the equality of souls was not a fundamental article of faith, though there have been many times when it must have been difficult to carry into practice. It cannot have been easy for a proud medieval prelate to believe sincerely that Jack Cade's soul was really equal with his own in the sight of God; and doctrines of election and many other exclusive dogmas have often gone dangerously near to establishing an aristocracy of souls. Christianity itself, however, built upon the life of a carpenter's son, has always been the religion of the Common Man and the hope of the Depressed Classes caught in the toils of status. The Lord's Prayer is the Common Man's prayer, and nothing is more insistent in the Gospels than condemnation of the Pharisaic sin of regarding one's own soul as better than the souls of other men. Frailties of the flesh could always look for mercy, but not this black sin of the spirit.

Equalitarian doctrines, however, were not confined to Christianity. Throughout the ages philosophers had pondered upon the inequalities among men, and especially upon the anomaly of slavery. The greatest of Roman jurists, Ulpian, anticipated Rousseau in laying down that by the Law of Nature all men were born free, though by the Law of Nations some were born slaves. Ulpian, however, had very little following in this doctrine, and the majority of Roman jurists did not distinguish between the Law of Nature and the Law of Nations. When, in the Christian era, the Law of Nature became the Law of God, Christianity accepted chattel slavery as an inevitable institution of society. Yet it was undoubtedly in the name of Christianity that Wilberforce and his followers led the crusade against slavery and, in the long run, expelled it from the Western world. This had become possible because, more than a century before, the Puritan congregations had made the junction between Christian and political equalitarianism. It was in the form of the Puritan 'priesthood of all believers' that political democracy first found its way to Massachusetts. Far south of it, men of faith like William Penn, Lord Baltimore, and General Oglethorpe, also sought new realms of liberty and toleration, and their idealism proved to be not merely 'starry-eyed'. The soil was fertile for Jefferson's version of Rousseauism when at last the seed, long stored, was ready to plant.

Thus the 'mystical' human soul of theology and philosophy became the 'literal' Common Man of democracy, and the world began to look forward to new possibilities instead of backwards to lost beatitudes. We hear much of this Common Man to-day. Since he shares in the government of himself and his fellows, we hope to find in him not merely the dignity of personality, but some measure of wisdom which fits him for rule. In the past he has, on the whole, been underrated by his intellectual 'betters'. To-day it is realized that he may have a faculty of judgement and a practical sagacity which are not to be measured in terms of examinations, certificates, and diplomas. The juryman is not usually as 'clever' a person as the learned judge and the learned counsel, but our law has not been misguided in believing that the juryman's point of view contributes something to the final issue which bewigged heads cannot always supply. Samuel Butler was far from being a Common Man; he was, indeed, one of the most uncommon men of the nineteenth century; but he never tired of insisting on the insufficiency of sheer reason to direct human affairs and on the ultimate necessity for a kind of intuitional wisdom which seems to have little relation to intellectual equipment. 'Cleverness' is too often merely a glibness of word and an idiom of wit; any dweller in the academic grove knows that it may be totally unrelated to any true discernment. He knows, too, that much which passes as 'learning', and which, by its mere phraseology would completely baffle the inarticulate Common Man, is not only sterile, but is really the product of a very inferior and unexacting mental process. Many a 'work of learning' is a far less imposing product of human activity than the handiwork of a good craftsman in the utilities of life. I do not know, and I suppose that nobody knows, how a brain works nor what composes its quality; but I am sure that its mere grey matter bears no necessary proportion to the contribution it can make to sensible human action. The rarest of gifts, and the true human wisdom, is to distinguish between the essential and the inessential in any given situation; and it is a gift which may be found in the humblest of men and may be lacking under the loftiest of brows.

These merits we can look for, or at least hope for, in the Common Man in a modern civilized community;

but we must not expect too much of him. I seem to detect in a good deal of present-day writing a tendency to depict him somewhat more than life-size. There was once an Economic Man, and he turned out to be a figment. We must beware lest our Common Man become a creature of romantic imagination. He has his manifest frailties. He is often the victim of his emotions. In situations which require not only dispassionate judgement, but close and sustained reasoning, he may be unequal to the effort. It is difficult for him to dissociate his judgement from his self-interest. Above all, when he merges into the Man of the Crowd, he is dangerously suggestible, especially under the mountainous impact of modern mechanical means of persuasion. He is neither hero nor cad, and all our calculations will err if we expect him invariably to behave as the one or the other. If I were looking for a far juster picture of him than I find in many political theorists, I should turn—again, no doubt, through personal predisposition—to the Average Reasonable Man of English law. But that is another story—a story based on centuries of acquaintance with him in every conceivable relationship of life.

PERSONAL RESPONSIBILITY OF THE INDIVIDUAL FOR
    GOVERNMENT

Democracy, then, must have common sense from the Common Man; and common sense may be found in the man who cannot read and write, just as it may be lacking in the man who can read and write in all the tongues of men and angels. But this does not mean that a man is *likely* to be wise because he cannot read or write. The probability is that he will be all the wiser if he has the opportunity of enlarging his know-

ledge and developing the muscles of his mind. Grace
is not at any man's command, but the means of grace
at least help towards salvation. All democratic systems, therefore, lay emphasis on education, with as
wide an extension as possible over all classes of society,
and with opportunities of advancement for those who
show capacity above the average. Education cannot,
of itself alone, make a good man or a wise man; but
it is a reasonable assumption that the spread of knowledge and the discipline of the intelligence will im-
prove the capacity of the average citizen for his frac-
tional share in self-government.

It goes without saying that this education must be
free. I do not mean free in the monetary sense; while
it is clear that a great measure of gratuitous education
must be available in a large community with varying
standards of wealth, I do not believe that all education of all grades should be obtainable without cost,
and I certainly do not believe that all education
should be standardized (as is now threatened in some
quarters) according to a Departmental pattern. There
is no virtue in mere quantity of teaching. I have the
greatest respect for American education, and some
little experience of it, but I fear that it has been too
easily assumed in the United States that the whole
problem of democratic intelligence can be solved by
merely distributing free education—or what passes
under that name—to everybody. A recent examination conducted by the *New York Times* among 7,000
college freshmen exhibited almost unbelievable ignorance of elementary facts of American history, and
caused much searching of heart about the whole
national policy in education. Mass-produced peda-
gogy is not education but the very antithesis of it, for

instead of training a mind to think, it fits it only, as a herd-mind, not to think.

But education must be free intellectually, for there is no bondage of mind or spirit more ruinous than the 'inspired' indoctrination of the young which is now practised by totalitarian systems. How far the State should exercise a censorship over educational methods and doctrines is a problem which involves the whole question of liberty of opinion; and that, for the moment, I postpone. There are a few schools in this country which, in the opinion of many, are admirably designed to turn out bad citizens. Most of us believe that it is better to let them try their experiments than to dragoon them; but however democratic a State were, there might well be a point beyond which eccentricity of education could not safely be allowed to go.

Spiritually, education exists for the good of the citizen's own individuality—the prime consideration of democracy; politically, it exists, or ought to exist, in order to strengthen his sense of responsibility to the community—in a word, to make him a better member of a better majority. Disaster must await a democracy in which the individual disclaims responsibility for his share in government. The inevitable result of that temper of mind is that government passes into the hands of professional politicians, and corruption and maladministration invariably follow. One of the most distressing features of modern France has been that many an average decent and intelligent citizen has regarded politics with distaste, often with contempt, and nearly always with resignation, as a game of low cunning for professional adventurers. From resignation he often passed to cynical detachment or impotent bitterness; what could he, a single unit, do against a whole system so deeply entrenched? One can sympathize with his helplessness and one may be as powerless as himself to suggest the infallible remedy; but what is certain is that once that disaccord has grown up between represented and representative, and once it has been accepted with supineness or despair, catastrophe is foredoomed. This problem of the weak elector and the powerful professional is a constant danger of representative systems. Nothing can solve it except a sanity of public opinion and a sense of personal responsibility which every means of education and self-cultivation must be used to promote.

Responsibility, and not solely privilege. The penalty of our great advances in 'social services' has been that too much emphasis has been laid on the claim of the individual on the community and too little on his own duty and power of contribution to it. In many of the Plans which now pullulate in a speculative post-war world there is the same disproportion. We all hope for a better world, but it certainly will not be an easy one, and it will not even be a better one without effort and cost from all according to capacity. The insistence on privilege without responsibility has undoubtedly been, in our generation, a weakness which has made it easy for false prophets to pour scorn on the 'flabbiness' of democracies and to issue ringing appeals to youth to chose the harder but more heroic way of service and sacrifice. While we believe that the price of that service as interpreted by Fascism is intolerable to the free individual, we should not underestimate the power of this appeal. It has always struck a more responsive chord than the invitation to comfort and indulgence. 'Take my yoke upon you' has been the call not only of Christianity, but of all great religious leaders.

Democracy, to be healthy, must offer not only re-wards, but tasks. Bentham misread human nature in supposing that man always desires pleasure and al-ways recoils from pain.

The sense of responsibility in British society has not been confined to the political sphere. No element in it has been more salutary than the amount and variety of voluntary service which has been given in every kind of social activity. It is unparalleled in the world. Not the least part of it has come from the so-called 'leisured' class which it is now the fashion to regard (so far as it survives) as an excrescence of drones and parasites. There is a real danger, in many of the plans which are now put forward, that much if not all of this unrewarded service may pass into the hands, in the name of 'organization', of Government officials. If this ever comes to pass, not only will democratic life suffer a grave decline of that very 'efficiency' which regimentation is intended to promote, but something vital will have gone out of the spirit of citizenship in this nation—an indispensable ingredient, as I believe, in the social cement of our particular kind of democracy.

REPRESENTATIVE GOVERNMENT AND FREE ELECTION

No modern democracy can, like that of Athens, place the final responsibility for government in the hands of the entire assembled people. Size and geo-graphy alone prevent this; but even if it were practic-able, would it be desirable? I believe not, because there is abundant warning evidence that man in the mass, especially under sinister influences, may easily become a creature of passion and not of reason. Democracy, in the 'mass' sense, always stands in danger of degenerating into what the Greeks called ochlocracy, or mob-government; and Greek history itself provided only too many examples of this tendency and its grievous consequences. All modern democracies therefore depend on representation based upon a wide franchise, and the expedient of the referendum has not proved successful except in small, compact communities; while the Dictators have repeatedly shown that the plebiscite, masquerading as the General Will, can, by cynical machination, be the very negation of democracy.

Three problems present themselves: (1) who are the best representatives? (2) how are they to be found? (3) what is their true function when they have been found?

(1) Theoretically, the representatives in a democratic state should be either of two groups; those members of the community who have been selected by their fellow-citizens for their conspicuous qualities of wisdom, probity, and leadership—a sort of Platonic aristocracy of natural rulers; or simply a 'cross-section' of average ability representing, as comprehensively as possible, all the different grades of interest, intelligence, and avocation in the community. We all know that in practice 'representative' assemblies do not answer exactly to either of these descriptions. No democratic State would seriously claim that its Lower Chamber consists entirely of a First Eleven of brains and virtue. Not only would a public of Common Men be extremely uncomfortable under such an esoteric rule, but (Plato notwithstanding) there is no adequate evidence that brains and virtue are in themselves sufficient for good government. Other and more earthy qualities are sometimes necessary, especially a

faculty for compromise which may not always accord with rigid principle or perfect logic. On the other hand, no democratic State would claim, or would wish to claim—indeed, it would resent the suggestion—that its Lower Chamber was like a jury selected by lot and consisting solely of average men. What a healthy democracy seems to get—at all events, in England and America—is an assembly consisting for the most part of men definitely above the average in talent, experience, and 'stake in the country', and for the rest, as to one small part, of men not above the average in any of these respects and, as to the smallest part of all, of men definitely pre-eminent in attainments, ambition, and leadership. I do not think that democracy can hope for a better blend than this, and it is impossible to lay down any invariable principles about the proportions of the ordinary and the extraordinary in the mixture, nor about the means by which it can be maintained. All must depend on the mysterious spirit called public opinion. As I have said, the greatest misfortune which can happen to a democracy is that decent average opinion should disinterest itself in the representative process and allow power to pass into the hands of professionals who use the democratic machinery only for their own ends.

A serious practical difficulty in modern communities is the age of the representative and his means of livelihood. In youth and middle age most men are establishing their position in life and can afford neither the time nor the energy for Parliamentary duties and for all the anxieties and exertions of elections. Financial independence becomes, and is likely in future to become, more and more rare as incomes dwindle under taxation and inherited wealth is diminished by death duties. Whatever collectivist arguments may be urged against a leisured class—however 'undemocratic' it may be considered—its extinction deprives democracy of a reservoir of representatives who have served it well in the past. The alternatives to it are either an Areopagus of elderly men who have made themselves financially secure by many years of hard and exhausting work, or the payment of a 'living wage', such as has been established in the United States, for all members. In England, we have adopted the compromise of paying an honorarium which can barely maintain those representatives who need it most, and which only covers, or helps to cover, the customary expenses and benevolences of those with independent incomes. It is not tempting enough in itself to have attracted, up to the present time, any very large class of those professional politicians, common enough in some countries, who 'live on the game'; and, fortunately, the tradition of British politics has, so far, discouraged the acquisition on any large scale of those ill-gotten gains which have accompanied professionalism in some democracies. The pressure, however, of economic equalitarianism, and the uncertainties of private and public economic conditions after the present war, raise grave doubts about the quality and aims of our representatives in the future. There have been loud complaints about the absence of youth from the ranks of our representatives and leaders in the inter-war years, and our Prime Minister is a man approaching the allotted span. Unhappily it cannot be claimed that where youth has been in command in other countries, during that period it has contributed notably to wise government or temperate ideals; but a democratic assembly is certainly the poorer if it does not

contain an adequate element of the younger generation. Nothing, on the other hand, could be worse for
democracy than a class of comparatively young men
who are attracted to politics by what they can get out
of it. It would be foolish to venture on prophecy, and
our race has not yet lost its gift for finding the middle
way; but it is difficult not to be perturbed by what
seem to be the probable alternatives of the future—
on the one hand, a considerable growth of the purely
professional class of politicians, with increased emolu-
ments and opportunties of profit, or, on the other
hand, a presbytery of elder statesmen ripe in experience and sober in judgement, but not readily responsive to the needs of changing times.

(2) The tendency of all modern democracy is towards universal suffrage. It took nearly a century,
even after the Reform Act, to complete itself in England. It is impossible to say that since the final stage
was reached the prestige of Parliament has increased
or that it has become more truly representative of the
will of the nation than it was fifty years ago. All are
agreed that its capacity for producing men of mark
has diminished, and that in the inter-war years our
policy and status suffered severely from this lack,
which the ravages of the first World War among our
'promising young men' are hardly sufficient to explain. Are these matters of pure coincidence? Has the
'flapper vote' really strengthened the hand of democracy? As an exhibition of democratic methods, a
general election in England, or a Presidential election
in the United States, is a depressing spectacle. With
a universal electorate the technique is nearly always
the same—to scale down the appeal to the lowest
intelligence, to substitute slogan and catchword for

reasoning, and to obscure the true issues under any sidewinds or irrelevancies which are likely to catch emotion and prejudice rather than reason. All party agents accept these methods as matters of course; a great many Common Men see through them, and either laugh at them or are irritated by them, but a great many other Common Men are deluded by them. Anybody who has ever attended a Party Convention in the United States needs all his faith to retain respect for government of the people, by the people, and for the people. Again, it is a commonplace to say that there are often, in modern societies, issues to be decided which the free and independent elector cannot really understand. The secrets and intricacies of foreign policy are hidden not only from the electorate but from Parliament itself, and sometimes even from members of the Government. How many Common, or even Uncommon, Men are qualified to judge of the best financial and fiscal policy for a country at a time of crisis? To a great many of us, the Gold Standard is a lugubrious joke. In the great crisis of 1931, the Government could only say: 'We cannot hope to explain this disease to you in terms which you will understand; if you trust us at all, you must trust us implicitly to find the best remedy we can; therefore, give us a Doctor's Mandate.' It was considered a high tribute to democracy that the patient was ready to submit, as an act of faith, to the treatment—and so, in some ways, it was; but it was a strange commentary on representative institutions.

Can democracy purge these derogations from its own dignity? When Mill discussed the question of the suffrage in 1861 (*Representative Government*) he was as emphatic that the vote should be universal (with a few obvious disqualifications) as that it should *not* be equal. He argued, on the one hand, that there could never be a widely diffused sense of political responsibility unless the suffrage was made available to all classes, and that the mere possession of the franchise was a powerful instrument of political education; and that the denial of it to any considerable number of persons (including women) must result not only in inertia but in grievance. On the other hand, he regarded 'one man one vote' as both illogical and mischievous, and advocated plural voting on a basis, not of property or of privilege, but of 'individual mental superiority'. It must be confessed, however, that he was vague and unconvincing about the qualifications of those who, through the exercise of 'superior functions', should be given plural voting power. His principal tests were occupational (according to the degree of responsibility and intelligence involved) and educational; but his proposals were merely tentative and he admitted that he was not prepared to give them 'a practical shape'—'nor should I wish to be bound by the particular proposals which I have made'. One could not envy the legislator who was confronted with the task of establishing the franchise on Mill's intellectual basis, and it is difficult to believe that it would be entertained by the prevailing democratic mood, which is distrustful, not without reason, of the 'high-brow'. The utmost that Mill could say of universal and equal suffrage was that he 'would not despair of it' if it secured proportional representation to minorities. He was so much attached to the notion of a graduated franchise that he did not think it even mattered greatly how many votes were vested in one individual, provided that the principle of graduation was maintained on such a basis 'as can be understood and accepted by the general conscience and understanding'. While he admired, and perhaps even over-rated, the educational effect of the universal suffrage in the United States, he deplored the conception and effects of the American doctrine 'that any one man (with a white skin) is as good as any other'. This creed he regarded as 'detrimental to moral and intellectual excellence'. There was nothing of 'literal' equality or of Rousseauism in Mill's democratic faith, ardent though it was.

Within the next half century, British democracy followed one of the paths which Mill had pointed out, but closed the other. A series of extensions made the franchise, for all practical purposes, universal, but, far from developing the principle of plural voting, legislation gradually abolished so much of it as already existed. To-day the University franchise is one of the few surviving examples of the plural vote. For what it is worth, it is based on Mill's intellectual qualification; but many are convinced that it is justified either in theory or by results, and its expectation of life seems to be precarious. I have already expressed doubt whether the power of the people, and the principles of representation combined with leadership, have grown in proportion to the spread of the suffrage; and I think it is equally open to question whether the vote has had that educational effect, and has given that stimulus to civic duty, which Mill hoped for it. The proportion of voters at any election is still surprisingly small. For many years the whole world was fascinated by the mingled comedy and tragedy of the struggle for woman's suffrage in England. Women not only bit and scratched and kicked, but died for the holy cause; men, too, martyred themselves; in the year 1913 I myself saw one of them nearly done to death by a mob. When at last the battle was won, the concession was made with the maximum of British illogicality—not as matter of right (which Mill had proclaimed it to be even in 1861), but as a Good Conduct Prize for loyal behaviour during a war. Is the right, so dearly won, now greatly prized, and has it contributed notably to the strength of democracy? Or has it been, like so many other things in life, valued above its worth in the seeking and below its worth in the attaining? Certainly it is not exercised with anything like the enthusiasm with which it was pursued, and there is little evidence that it has influenced political trends either for better or for worse. Women have shown no great desire to send representatives of their own sex to Westminster and those few who have been chosen have not added eminently to the counsels of the nation, though it is only fair to say that they have not been below the average of the opposite sex. In the United States, they have been no more numerous or remarkable. This is not said by way of reproach or criticism, and is certainly not meant to suggest that, if the suffrage is to be universal, women have not an equal right to it with men; but it does give cause for doubt whether the *mere* generality of voting power will, as Mill seems to have believed, breed a sense of political responsibility.

Is any 'filter' of universal suffrage possible? In the abstract, the notion of indirect election has much to commend it. With the object of finding the best representatives in a crowded community, what could be more sensible, in theory, than to appoint electors who, both by their own proved qualities and by the

c

comparative paucity of their numbers, will be in a far
better position to make a calm and judicious choice
than the emotional masses? This, again, was an idea
which Mill carefully reviewed, and his habitual common sense at once detected its two dangerous weaknesses. It was, he said, too much to expect of the
ordinary human nature of democracy that men would
be content to discharge this important selective function in a spirit of perfect detachment. The ideal
electors of this type would need 'a zeal for what is
right in the abstract, an habitual principle of duty for
the sake of duty, which is possible only to persons of
a rather high grade of cultivation, who, by the very
possession of it, show that they may be and deserve
to be, trusted with political power in a more direct
shape'. The other danger, even more realistic, was the
corruption and intrigue to which a small body of
electors, unless men of singular probity, might be
exposed. Mill's conclusion, therefore, was that indirect
election was practicable only if the electors had some
other important function to perform in the constitutional system; and he cited as a successful example of
this method the selection of senators in America by
the State legislatures.

The few experiments which democracy has made in
indirect election have shown Mill's fears to have been
well-founded. Even the one instance which he singled
out for admiration proved to be impermanent. The
constant pressure of 'democratic' opinion led, in 1913,
to the Seventeenth Amendment of the Constitution,
by which the election of senators was transferred from
the State legislatures to popular vote, and, as is well
known, it now takes place simultaneously with the
election of members of the House of Representatives.

If the change has not improved the quality and status of members of the Senate (and I know of no evidence that it has done so), it does not, on the other hand, appear to have lowered it, and the Senate still remains by far the more influential of the two chambers in the United States. A much more conspicuous example of the failure of the indirect method was one which had long been visible even in Mill's day, though, strangely enough, it did not attract his notice. The framers of the American constitution gave specially anxious thought to the method of electing the President. It was considered essential that he should be a person pre-eminent in character and ability, lest the large powers vested in him should become either a fiction or an autocracy. The device adopted was that of electoral colleges in each State, appointed by popular election, and equal in number to the representatives which the State sent to Congress. The electors were intended to be entirely impartial persons, not themselves members of Congress, nor the holders of any federal office—in short, men with no axe to grind in the selection of the best qualified person for the highest function in the community. The founders believed that they had really solved the problem, and, as we may learn from *The Federalist*, there was no part of their handiwork of which they were more proud than this ingenious and attractive expedient. But almost from the first it broke down. The nomination of George Washington was practically uncontested and the electors had an easy task; but with the third Presidential campaign in 1796 the electors rapidly degenerated into party representatives. They have remained so ever since and to-day they are no more than conduit-pipes of a popular vote canvassed and registered on party lines. Not only has the intention of the constitution been frustrated, but the strange result is a Presidential election which, though popular, is neither direct nor indirect. Since the actual, final election is by States, it may happen, and indeed it has happened, that, with the great disparity of populations in the various States, a President may be elected by a minority of the total number of voters throughout the nation.

Were there any data, it would be interesting to speculate whether the average quality of American Presidents would have been better or worse than it has in fact been if the original intention of the constitution had been fulfilled; but, since the experiment has never really been made, there is no evidence on which to base any conclusions. Nor is much evidence to be found among other modern democracies. The French constitution provides a somewhat elaborate example of the indirect method in the election of the senate, which is appointed by electoral colleges consisting, in each Department, of the Deputies for that division, sitting with representatives from the Councils of the Department, of the *arrondissements*, and of the *communes*. Opinions differ about the success of the system. If the intention of the constitution was to ensure a special quality of gravity and statesmanship in the Second Chamber, it has not been realized in any marked degree. The Senate has played a respectable, but hardly a distinguished, part in French politics, its main usefulness being the negative function of a brake on hasty or intemperate action. Even this merit, in the opinion of some observers, has been dearly bought at the cost of the intrigue (not to put it any lower) which is said to surround the collegiate elections.

It would seem, then, that a 'filter' of the popular vote, even if it be approved in theory, is difficult to establish on any satisfactory basis, and that it is not acceptable to modern democratic sentiment. My own belief is that it has not yet received as much attention as it deserves from democracy, and that, in the abstract the principles laid down by Mill still hold good; but I must confess to feeling almost insuperable difficulty in applying them or in suggesting any standard by which plural voting could be made to commend itself to an electorate now wedded to the dogma of 'one man to count as one and not more than one'. Since politics is 'the art of the possible', little is to be gained by advocating methods which have no practical chance of attainment; and we are therefore thrown back on hopes that democracy will, by its own evolution, abate the grave weaknesses which now mar the popular vote and the means of wooing it. It is manifest that such hopes can be realized only by the progressive raising and strengthening of the average intelligence, vitality, and civic sense of the individual—a process in which education must play the leading part.

(3) Democracy presents the eternal paradox, which gives an easy handle to its critics, that in all the most important issues of government the representative assembly, in order to be efficient, ceases to exercise any representative function. There is no greater issue which any nation has to decide than that of peace or war. Nobody suggests that it should be submitted to a referendum; it is not even submitted to the representative assembly itself. In many great issues of national policy, a government constantly has to take responsibilities which it would not dare to refer to

popular decision; and during a time of emergency, it is, for all practical purposes, autocratic.

Nobody nowadays holds the theory of the literal 'mandate', or believes that the representative is merely a gramophone record of His Master's Voice. Burke put the position, as long ago as 1774, to the electors of Bristol, in words which have been constantly quoted:

'Parliament is not a congress of ambassadors from different and hostile interests; which interests each must maintain, as an agent and advocate, against other agents and advocates; but Parliament is a deliberative assembly of one nation, with one interest, that of the whole; where not local purposes, not local prejudices ought to guide, but the general good, resulting from the general reason of the whole. You choose a member indeed; but when you have chosen him, he is not member of Bristol, but he is a member of Parliament.'

While Burke believed this to be the picture of true representative government, Rousseau interpreted it to mean that the British citizen was free only at the time of a general election, and thereafter was a political slave. We know that to be as untrue as it would be false to suggest that the elector is 'represented' in the sense that he has constant control over the thoughts and actions of his representative. We fall back on the principle that, if public opinion is healthy, democracy will put into power citizens who, deciding collectively in any of the innumerable situations which cannot be precisely foreseen, will act in a manner which reflects the general, informed and deliberate spirit of the majority of the citizens. And again we must emphasize that unless that indefinable *rapport* exists between the body of electors and the individuals which it chooses,

Parliamentary government becomes merely the play-
ground of personal ambitions and of what Burke calls
'different and hostile interests'.

LEADERSHIP

A democracy, however, cannot be either vigorous
or secure if its representative assembly is a mere
sounding-board. It is already a common and sometimes a bitter criticism of the democratic system that
its representatives constantly govern their actions not
by their own true judgement but by that which will
look well in the constituency. To the *blasé* politician
the two supreme abominations are either 'This will
lose me a hundred votes' or 'There are no votes in
this'. A blizzard of telegrams to Congressmen is one
of the favourite methods of 'pressure groups' in
America; whether it has the intimidating effect which
is intended, or whether it defeats itself by over-
emphasis, I am not qualified to say. One of the com-
monest strictures on our government in the past
generation, especially in the matter of rearmament,
has been that our leaders did not lead and did not
make sufficient effort to 'educate public opinion'. The
constant cry has been: 'We did not put these men in
power merely to echo us, to soothe us, or even to
please us; we elected them to guide us, to inform us,
to warn us, and if necessary to demand unpleasant
duties of us.' Those who are now most emphatic in
these reproaches seldom stop to inquire whether warn-
ings would have been heeded and whether the democratic public would have continued to follow exponents of the unpalatable truths which are so evident
in retrospect.

The representative is always in the difficulty that if

he is too far in advance of public opinion, and if he administers too many shocks, he may lose all further opportunities of 'educating' his public, for the excellent reason that his public will throw him out of office. It may be heroic to become a voice crying in the wilderness, but it is not practically effective. It is not, therefore, always mere cowardice which prevents the politician from announcing, in blunt terms, what he really believes if he knows that it will be unpopular; he often has to consider how he can lead public opinion without letting it become aware that it is being led. The process is not only exceedingly delicate but often painfully slow, and to a statesman of strong judgement it must often tax patience almost beyond endurance. In modern times there is no more remarkable example of it than Mr. Roosevelt's handling of public opinion before America's entry into the war.

The dangers and complexities of this process, and the slowness of its tempo, are absurd and intolerable in totalitarian theory. Reaction against its chafing fetters has been in no small measure responsible for the cult of what Sir Ernest Barker (*Reflections on Government*) calls 'the emergent individual'. But there is something deeper here than revolt against the trammels and delays of the democratic process: for all dictatorship is based on the theory of the Uncommon Man. It necessarily repudiates the idea of 'representation', for it is of the essence of the Leader that he is *not* representative, but far above all others in quality and capacity and even in some mystic power which is almost superhuman. This is the very reason of his mission. True, he is supposed to be the personification of the soul and purpose of a people, and in that sense he is 'representative' of it; but it is not for any Common Man, who values his life or liberty, to question the interpretation which the Leader may put upon national or personal destiny. A great deal of German thought, for many a long day, has been groping towards this Giant Man; what it has never clearly envisaged is the means by which he emerges, and how he is to be kept within bounds, and saved from the corruption of absolute power, once he has emerged.

How far does democracy encourage, or even tolerate, the Emergent Individual? The English, it is said, distrust politicians who are 'too clever', and in some of the newer British civilizations it would almost seem that to be conspicuously above the average in education and intelligence is a positive disadvantage in politics. Nevertheless, I believe it to be true that the vitality of a democracy is to be judged largely by its capacity to produce leaders and to find the Man for the Moment.

We need not go back to Pericles, though his name at once springs to the mind; we can see the Emergent Individual clearly enough in the first and now the oldest of modern democracies. As we have seen, the quality of the American Presidents has, on the average, been disappointing by comparison with the pains which the Constitution took to safeguard it; but it is remarkable how at every great crisis in American history, the individual seems to have emerged. This cannot be pure chance; there seems to be something in the democratic system, and the responsibilities which it imposes, which can make a man greater than himself. The Greeks had a proverb: 'Office shows the man.' *Office*, not power; and office, by derivation, is a sort of service; a dictator does not 'hold office'. Lincoln was fifty-one when he was elected President; up to that time his career had been, if not one of actual failures and discouragements, certainly undistinguished. The mere election of the 'rail-splitter' was an insult and a challenge to the Southern gentleman. It is one of the marvels of literature where this rough-hewn man, who is said to have had only one whole day's schooling and most of whose life had been spent in circumstances of mental and physical crudity, acquired a power of language which can, to this day, stir men's hearts and minds. Who, again, could have discerned in the conventional, humdrum squire of Mount Vernon a General who could, by sheer tenacity as much as by native shrewdness in the field, lead an ill-equipped and undisciplined force, at the head of a nation far from united, to victory against a great Power? In our own day, Mr. Roosevelt, until he went to the White House, except for one severe physical misfortune, had sailed with fair winds upon smooth waters; competent though he was in all duties which fell to him, he had never been pitted against the hurricane, and few detected in him the supreme navigator and great captain which he proved to be in the hour of the storm. We may come nearer home. It is no disrespect to Mr. Churchill to say that since, late in life and after many disappointments, he has been called to the highest office, he seems to have grown to a new stature. He has displayed qualities of gravity, of bigness and, above all, of patience which have not always been evident in him—qualities, indeed, of which, but a short time ago, many of his critics would have declared him constitutionally incapable. Office, its bitters as well as its sweets, shows the man.

And yet none of these men was ever the 'emergent'

Superman or the deified dictator. They, and all their kind, have been the martyrs as well as the darlings of democracy. None has escaped criticism, frustration, or bitter hostility; one of those whom I have named died at the assassin's hand, and all have died many deaths in the implacable minds of their opponents. I observed not long ago that a politician declared it an admirable example of democracy that the Duke of Wellington had his windows broken. Perhaps it was equally admirable that William Pitt so long remained in the wilderness while his fellow-countrymen, like those of a century later, tried to anaesthetize hard realities with wishful thinking. The cruelties, ingratitudes, and caprices of popular sentiment are a sad commentary on the General Will; but they are at least the price, heavy but not intolerable, of restraint on personal power. No democratic statesman is so deluded as to be unconscious of them; and though, no doubt, personal pre-eminence is, to some men, worth almost any cost, to a man of realistic sense the extreme precariousness of power, and the risks of injustice, misrepresentation, and ingratitude—those bitterest of medicinal draughts —make democratic leadership no less a cross than a prize. Under such restraints, neither ambition nor sheer ability will suffice without a dominant sense of duty. Democracy, if sound, must produce not only the democratic ordinary man, but the democratic extraordinary man. He must command and he must serve, in one and the same motion; and there are few tasks which require higher gifts both of mind and of character. It is true that his freedom of judgement and action are often hampered by the exigencies of service; seldom, in politics, can a statesman go straight ahead for the objective on which he has decided, for

there are always qualifications to be made in defer-
ence to this or that interest or body of opinion. He is
always compromising and reconciling, and to a man
of strong will and clear vision these restraints must
often be irksome beyond bearing. They are the more
so because it is often impossible for him to explain
himself as fully as he could do if the public interest
did not often demand silence. Once again the Totalitarian pours scorn upon checks and balances, deeming
it absurd and mischievous that the true leader should
be hampered in pace and policy by restraints which
his judgement rejects. In democratic theory, however,
this type of patience is utterly essential to the leader;
it is axiomatic that his sole judgement, however powerful, is never a sufficient foundation of policy. The
resulting inconveniences are often grave, but they are
not too high a price for the vital principle of service
linked with power. The President of the United States
possesses, by the constitution, remarkably extensive
powers, and in time of war they are almost startling
in their scope; but any President who is chronically at
loggerheads with Congress has ceased to be the leader
of the nation, and it is not the least of Mr. Roosevelt's
political achievements that, though constantly accused
by his enemies of 'dictatorship', he has, so far, avoided
that deadlock, which was so disastrous to Woodrow
Wilson. Mr. Churchill is not the most submissive of
men, and there have been times in his career when
he has stood solitary in the attitude of defiance; but,
since he has held the highest responsibility in the
gravest hour, he has never departed from the principle
that he is at all times the servant of the House of
Commons. This is sincere democratic instinct; but it
is also astute policy; for, as an old Parliamentarian,

he well knows that if he once departed from that position, his influence with the House would be gone. There is nothing about which the House of Commons is more jealous. On 8 June 1943 Mr. Churchill gave to the House of Commons a narrative of achievements in which a note of personal complacency might have been pardonable. It was no mere rhetoric, but the authentic voice of democracy, which spoke in his concluding words:

'Let me record the fact that this House, a democratic institution based upon universal suffrage which has preserved its function and authority intact and undiminished during the war, and has shown it can change, correct, and sustain Governments with equal constancy of purpose, has proved itself the foundation and instrument for the waging of successful war and for the safety of the State never surpassed in modern or ancient times.'

Since no two men are alike, it is impossible to define the qualities which a democratic community looks for in its leaders, still less to define that particular quality, or combination of qualities, which constitutes 'appeal to the popular imagination'. The British public loves and hates all manner of different men and characters, but, on the whole, while its Puritan elements disapprove the openly disreputable, it resembles poor Queen Guinevere in preferring Sir Lancelot to King Arthur, for it loves 'a touch of earth'. All one can say is that democracy, if it is to survive, must produce the Uncommon Man who understands and serves the Common Man, with all his weaknesses and strengths. As Mr. Lindsay has put it: 'A modern democratic state is only possible if it can combine appreciation of skill, knowledge, and expertness' (and may we not add character and personality?) 'with a reverence for the common humanity of everyday people.' There has been no more significant symptom of the sickness of modern French democracy than its failure to produce true leaders and great personalities; and we ourselves have had no small cause for anxiety on the same score in the past twenty years.

THE MAJORITY PRINCIPLE

'The majority,' cried Dr. Stockmann in Ibsen's *Enemy of the People*, 'is never right!

'Never, I say! That is one of those conventional lies against which a free, thoughtful man must rebel. Who are they that make up the majority of a country? Is it the wise men or the foolish? I think we must agree that the foolish folk are, at present, in a terribly overwhelming majority all around and about us the wide world over. But, devil take it, it can surely never be right that the foolish should rule over the wise! Yes, yes, you can shout me down, but you cannot gainsay me. The majority has might—unhappily—but right it has not. I and a few others are right. The minority is always right!'

The most ardent democrat would hardly claim that the majority is always right—certainly not by any absolute standard of truth and error, wisdom and unwisdom. Democracy claims, first, that the majority, right or wrong, is entitled to have its way; and second, that on the whole, though with many exceptions, majority opinion does reach a sensible and workable solution of most of the practical problems of social life—that the common sense of the Common Man can be trusted, in most situations, to remain sensible and to find expedients which will work better than the devices and desires of pure intelligence or Olympian wisdom.

The first of these principles requires, as it seems to me, little analysis or justification. There is much discussion about the ethical basis of majority rule—whether, for example, it rests on the force or coercion which is applied by sheer weight of numbers. I think the answer is that the will of the majority is the only practical means by which any association of human beings can be made to work, and I should not be afraid of the principle that, in the last resort, it is made to work by superior might. That would be an alarming thought if it meant that the will of the majority must in all cases be imposed on minorities by the Big Stick; but it is the essence of democracy that this does not normally happen, since, as we shall see, the will of the majority is not merely arbitrary domination, but, as nearly as possible, major opinion qualified by a great variety of minor dissents. If, however, difference of view is, on any essential principle, irreconcilable, then there is no course open but resort to coercion, and either rebellion or civil war is the result. It is a testimony to the average efficacy of the democratic method that this *ultima ratio* has been rare, and it is perhaps not without significance that its most conspicuous and most tragic example in the nineteenth century—the American Civil War—arose out of a principle fundamental to the whole fibre of democracy, that of human liberty.

The will of the majority is not only a commonplace in the daily affairs of us all, but is really inherent in all systems of government whatsoever. Not even despotism can ignore it. Sir Henry Maine long since exploded the popular conception of the Oriental potentate as completely absolute and arbitrary; he is, in fact, usually far more in bondage to custom and tradition than the constitutional monarch, and very often his personal power is negligible. There is no ruler on earth who is raised to a higher point of deification than the Emperor of Japan, and none with less power in the State. True, the real engrossers of power in a despotic system are often an oligarchy, caste, or priesthood; but always there is the possibility of a Secession of the Plebs, which cannot be disregarded even by the modern Dictator with all the tanks and machine guns at his command, for he knows in his heart that in the end not even these can prevail against the spirit of man. Even the exponents of absolute sovereignty, not excluding Austin, recognized the 'fear of revolution' as an extra-constitutional limitation on sovereignty, whether they condemned it, like Hobbes, as a breach of the Social Contract, or justified it, like Locke, as a term of it. (Even Hobbes hesitatingly admitted that there were some sovereign commands which the subject would be justified in disobeying.) Herbert Spencer ('The Great Political Superstition' in *The Man versus the State*) offered a new version of the social contract, and one which it is surprising to find in the nineteenth century. The fallacy, he urged, of majority rule (which he feared would become the greatest of all tyrannies) was its assumption that the individual consented to abide by the decision of the majority in all matters without exception. On the contrary, said Spencer, there were some things in which any reasonable man would be prepared to accept the majority opinion, and others in which he had never consented, and possibly never would consent, to do anything of the kind. Spencer took as an illustration the position of a shareholder with regard to the memorandum and articles of a commercial company. The choice of this example is sufficient in itself to show the artificiality of Spencer's reasoning, and indeed of most theories of the social contract. There is no analogy, except by way of imperfect metaphor, between the agreement of a shareholder or other voluntary contractor and the position of the citizen in society. The insuperable difference is that the individual is not born, and does not become a member of a particular community, of his own free will. Figures of speech apart, it is contrary to plain fact to conceive him as formulating or assenting to the terms on which he is prepared to become a citizen. He does not do so, as the satirist has said, 'in spite of all temptations, To belong to other nations', and he does not enter into a 'lease of life' in his cradle. The conditions of the so-called 'contract' are, for the most part, predetermined, and therefore the notion of his agreeing to this or that condition of government, at the very moment when he becomes subject to government, is mere fiction. This, however, does not mean that for the rest of his life he is the mere slave of the State, reduced to the Old Order of immutable status, and without any independence of action or judgement; it means only that his freedom is exercised within a certain social periphery which is not of his own choosing, and which, if he dislikes it, he can either try to alter by constitutional means or exchange for another nationality, when he has reached maturity. Though he remains free to dissent to the utmost in his opinions, in matters of conduct his freedom can never go to the point of rejecting and resisting the will of the majority on the ground (which is false in fact) that he never

D

undertook to accept it. Thus the 'agreement to differ' is, in one sense, an agreement only by courtesy, since it is involuntary. But in another and a very important sense it is voluntary, and morally justifiable, because it is a principle of behaviour which the average reasonable man learns, of his own judgement, to approve and to adopt. Unless he is a bigot or an exhibitionist, John Styles's own experience teaches him, in the famous words of Cromwell, to 'think it possible he may be mistaken', or, even when he is not convinced of that (and some people are extremely difficult to convince of the mere possibility), to concede that degree of compromise which alone can prevent social life from becoming 'the war of every man upon every man'. If he is neither convinced nor ready to concede, then there is nothing for him but coercion. This is average reasonable behaviour the world over, wherever men are capable of forming opinions of their own; but I think it can be claimed without complacency that in a democratic community men learn more easily than elsewhere to agree to differ, and that the very process of agreement implies that concession is voluntary and not made at the wholesale sacrifice of individual judgement.

Whatever interpretation, then, we place on the General Will, or even if we prefer not to add to its many and confusing interpretations, we can agree that no system of government can really work if it violates the sentiments or habits of the majority of the governed (which is not the same proposition as the fiction of the 'consent of the governed'), and that in that sense the majority not only does but must have its way in the long run. The second principle is much more dubious. Is the majority generally right—not right in the abstract, ethical sense, but right as representing the general sense of the community concerning action and policy in any given situation? Has the majority the right not only to be right, but to be wrong?

Reason revolts from the notion that mere quantity of opinion can give it any property of rightness or wisdom, especially in view of the many means of mass-suggestion and base appeal which show democracy at its worst. We have noticed, too, the kind of false unanimity which can be produced by managed plebiscites in totalitarian States. If quantity were all, the majority principle would be unattractive indeed. But it is the hope and the intent of the democratic method that the prevailing opinion shall represent a quality as well as a quantity—indeed, that its quantity should exist only for the sake of a quality. As Sir Ernest Barker has expressed it:

'Nor is the cause of Democracy a cause of number. It is not the worship of quantity: it is the worship of a quality—that quality of the thinking and discoursing mind which can dare to raise and to face conflicting views of the Good, and to seek by the way of discussion some agreed and accepted compromise whereby a true (because general) national will is attained, as it cannot otherwise be, and a national Good is secured which is really good because it is freely willed.'

It is, perhaps, an idealistic assumption that what emerges out of the majority opinion is necessarily a Good; I would repeat that the majority has the right to be wrong, but in so far as the result is 'freely willed' it partakes, *eo ipso*, of the nature of the Good. There is scarcely any political or social question on which conflicting views may not be held, and, in a democratic society, will not be held. We can look back to-day on many reforms in the nineteenth century which seem to us such imperative measures of progress that we marvel that they can ever have been contested. Yet every one of them was bitterly opposed and the men who opposed them were, in many cases, no less sincere than the reformers. It would be difficult to find a single intelligent person to-day who would defend the institution of slavery; but we should do a grave injustice if we imagined that everybody who fought against Lincoln or Wilberforce was actuated solely by self-interest, inhumanity, or stupidity. Granted, as all democracies must grant, the right of free speech, the conflicting views never lack means of expression, and out of the clash there nearly always comes a compromise, or at least a modification, which creates a *modus vivendi*. In this manner the majority opinion takes on a quality which, though it is not representative of the whole—for that is impossible in any society—is representative of a composite quality of the whole. The majority has become less positive or less arbitrary than it was, and the minority, though usually still unconvinced, can at least accept the situation without intolerable sacrifice of principle. It cannot always be so; it was not so in America in the very case of slavery; but in England, in the same instance, majority opinion prevailed after a series of compromises extending over nearly half a century. This was characteristic, for very often the majority opinion, which naturally believes itself to represent 'progress', has to administer its medicine in homeopathic doses. Hence the 'time-lag', so exasperating to the reformer who has no doubts about the efficacy of his remedies and his policies. Such a one was Jeremy Bentham, of whom Mill said that he was prepared to treat the whole of history as a blank page and start again at the beginning. Even at the cost, which is sometimes heavy enough, of the time-lag, this method is inadmissible in a democracy, and is, indeed, inimical to its whole spirit. The mills of public opinion grind slowly, but in the end they grind exceeding small. Substitute for them an up-to-date, labour-saving, mass-production, electrical mill of high voltage, and you have taken an essential vitamin out of the bread of democracy. What a number of these high-powered, mechanical mills we have nowadays whirling out the Bread of Life for the post-war World!

If democracy is to preserve the representative quality in the principle of majority-quantity, it follows that it must not only permit, but must encourage, diversity of opinion and individuality. *E pluribus unum* was a good motto not only for a political federation, but for a young democratic community vigorous in thought and action; and it has never been abandoned in the United States. Unanimity of opinion, even if it possessed any merit in itself, is manifestly impossible among any assembly of sentient human beings. A State often has to *act* unanimously, but the democratic State does so not on the basis that everybody is in perfect accord, but that everybody has agreed to differ, and, differing, to act in the interests of the whole. All totalitarian States, on the other hand, proceed on the assumption either that everybody thinks unanimously, or that if anybody differs, he is automatically wrong and shall not be suffered to express his error in word or deed. The one assumption is palpably false and the other, to the democratic mind, demonstrably pernicious. Either may succeed for a time, but to believe that it can succeed for ever is to abandon all faith in human dignity and destiny.

Another corollary of the majority-principle, properly interpreted, is that those who have agreed to differ shall be entitled to respect and consideration from those whose opinion has prevailed. We call this the doctrine of the 'rights of minorities'. The term 'rights' is here to be taken cautiously. The minority has no right to refuse action or duty which the majority has clearly willed. To admit this would be to negate the whole agreement to differ. The minority is entitled to maintain its dissent and to enjoy such exceptions and concessions as the majority can permit it without endangering the general policy which has been adopted. Above all, the minority can continue to express its disagreement and advocate its views, in the hope of converting itself from a minority into a majority; for it is of the essence of democracy that the minorities of to-day are the majorities of to-morrow, just as it is a commonplace of history that revolutions are nearly always the work of active minorities. What limits democracy can legitimately set to non-conformity of opinion, as well as of conduct, will be considered presently.

Throughout this discussion, I am conscious that it is all too easy to speak of majorities and minorities; but are we quite clear what *is* a majority or a minority in democracy? Each has its dangers and its contradictions. If the majority opinion is to prevail, its justification must be that it is *real* opinion 'freely willed', after due consideration of all the diversities of opinion. But majority opinion has a dangerous tendency towards auto-suggestion. It can inflate itself with its own breath and blow up its brain into a bladder of wind. In the very infancy of American democracy, Tocqueville perceived this danger. He wrote: 'In the principle of equality I very clearly discern two tendencies; the one leading the mind of every man to untried thoughts, the other inclined to prohibit him from thinking at all. And I perceive how, under the dominion of certain laws, democracy would extinguish the liberty of the mind to which the democratic social condition is favourable; so that, after having broken all the bondage once imposed on it by ranks or by men, the human mind would be closely fettered to the general will of the greatest number.'

With all the compliments that we may pay to the Common Man, we must not overrate his power of thinking for himself. That is a task which none of us finds easy—indeed, in many matters it is impossible. If we have not personal knowledge or experience—and in an enormous variety of matters we cannot possibly have them—we must accept them from others; we are 'a part of all that we have met', but also a part of all that we have heard and learned and read, and only a very small fraction of our equipment is really 'first-hand'. If a thousand people are saying the same thing at the same time, we cannot fail to be impressed by it; it slips imperceptibly into our consciousness, and it is only a rare individual who will question 'what I tell you three times' and think it all out for himself from the beginning. Even if he does, he is greatly reinforced in his own opinion by finding it supported and applauded. To think with the majority is the line of least resistance, and to dissent from it requires not only independence of mind, but courage, above the average. Our Common Man tends very easily to become the Man of the Crowd, to whom there is no greater bugbear than to be heterodox. It is the usual experience that the more ready-made an opinion is, the more intolerant it is—the more unreasoning, the more positive. This is the 'valour of ignorance' against which all democracies need to be on their guard. It is the 'slave-morality' of Nietzsche, and if Tocqueville were alive to-day it would be interesting to know which of the two adversaries, regimentation or originality, seemed to him to have prevailed in the maturity of popular government.

There is danger, too, that the majority may not be a majority at all, either in quantity or in quality, but the artificial creation of a minority. Again and again it is proved that the active minority can impose its will on the apathetic majority. Democracy, after all, is not merely a doctrine or a theory—it is a system of government with complicated machinery, and the adroit, unscrupulous, or determined manipulation of that machinery may lead to results which bear little or no relation to a General Will. The 'pressure group' is a constant and a formidable element in American politics, and it can do remarkable things. It is now generally agreed that it imposed Prohibition upon a nation, if not against its will, certainly not as the result of any genuine majority desire. A convinced few can often present the indifferent many with an accomplished fact before the many have realized the nature of the fact, and this is always the easier when the few arrogate to themselves a righteousness which it is not quite respectable to oppose, however spurious it may be, It is remarkable how many doctrinaire minorities find themselves on the side of the angels, and what ready and powerful, not to say promiscuous, allies the angels are. In England, Mrs. Grundy is everybody's butt and every politician's dread. She may be a minority of one, and she may be a very drab old lady, but singularly few Hon. Members dare to go into the lobby against her. She maintains, for example, betting laws and Sabbath laws which it would be fantastic to pretend are the real will of the majority of English people.

These mischiefs are not confined to democratic societies, but are universal among men. While democracy regretfully admits them, recognizing, if it is wise, that they are weaknesses to be watched and corrected, the total State attempts to eliminate them by placing all power and all rightness in the hands of one or of a few. The dangers of that desperate solution are manifestly greater than those of the disequilibrium of majorities and minorities. As against the tyranny either of mass-opinion or of fanatical minorities there is no true remedy except the constant cultivation, which every democracy desires, of the average intelligence of the individual; from that source, and that alone, can come independence of judgement. Mass-suggestion and blind orthodoxy there will always be among men, but on the whole it cannot be said of the democracies either of America or of Britain that they have been lacking in men of original minds who dared, in Tocqueville's words, 'untried thoughts'. What has been said of political leadership is equally true of intellectual leadership; no democracy is fully realizing itself unless its free atmosphere produces uncommon out of common thought and knowledge. This it did in nineteenth-century England and America with a great wealth of originality in literature, art, and science. There is cause for uneasiness in the fact that the twentieth century has not done so in anything like the same degree, except in the scientific sphere.

There still remains the question of the ethical and intellectual *right* of the majority to rule. Dr. Stockmann is still crying, 'The majority is never right!' In effect, the dictators are saying this too. They are saying: 'You, the common herd, are not capable of thinking for yourselves; it is only uncommon men who can do that. We are uncommon men, and we will do the thinking for you, and then persuade you that you have thought for yourselves what we tell you to think.' The strength of the argument is that the blood of the martyrs is the seed of progress. Posterity repeatedly honours the men whom their contemporaries crucified, and without rebels and heretics human intelligence would have stagnated. In short, it is only those who have opposed and defied the majority who have, in the long run, led and converted the majority. This is the hard law of wisdom—truth may be great, and it may prevail, but the field of history is strewn with its victims. Dr. Stockmann, then, justly concludes that the minority is always right? It does not follow, and it manifestly is not so, if we think of certain minorities; but it must be confessed that for every intelligent man there are moments when he feels that an opinion has only to be held widely enough, and to be repeated often enough, to excite his scepticism. The very fact of its automatic acceptance rouses suspicions that it is the opinion of Echo rather than of Ego.

But a society which is composed solely of rebels is a contradiction in terms, unless we are to go back to Hobbes's (wholly unscientific) picture of the society of unmitigated strife. Unanimity, we are agreed, is impossible, but some degree of conformity every community must demand not only in conduct but even in opinion; and the anxious problem for democracy is how much nonconformity it can safely permit. In England, we flatter ourselves that anybody can express any opinion about anything. But that is not the law. Few people realize that it is a criminal offence for any person who has been educated in, or at any time made profession of, the Christian religion 'by writing, printing, teaching, or advised speaking, to deny the Christian religion to be true, or the Holy Scriptures of the Old and New Testament to be of Divine authority'; and the penalty upon a second conviction for this offence is remarkable—it is not only three years' imprisonment, but deprivation of nearly all civic rights, even to the power of making a will. It is also a misdemeanour to 'deprave, despise, or contemn' the Lord's Supper or the Book of Common Prayer. It appears to be an offence 'to excite contempt and hatred against the Church by law established'. It is a crime to 'bring into hatred or contempt' the government and constitution of the United Kingdom, as by law established. Severe restrictions, these—if they were ever enforced. From the statutes (some of them dating back to Elizabeth) which impose them I turn to a newspaper, where I find a Member of Parliament reported as using these expressions at a public meeting: 'Churchill has collected in London an army of cowardly runaway generals and politicians from foreign lands, Labour Gauleiters and trade union Quislings. This collection of renegades have decided to continue the war with the bodies of workers. The workers are goaded on by another force of Communist gangsters who disgrace the name of Communism.' These words are spoken in the midst of war, when extraordinary restraints are imposed on free speech; but nobody prosecutes the speaker for bringing the government into hatred and contempt, because the common sense of democracy dislikes making martyrs of mere ranters. Nevertheless, the power to restrain ranting, if it is dangerous and not merely absurd, is always kept in reserve.

The classic case of democratic nonconformity is Socrates. There is much in his philosophy, and in his defence of it, which it is difficult to admire. It is neither a very noble nor a very convincing attitude to say, on the one hand, 'The Delphic Oracle has pronounced me the wisest man alive, and, moreover, I have a *daimon* which always tells me when I am right,' and, on the other hand, 'I am therefore the humblest of men, and I know nothing—but, anyhow, I know more than you!' One cannot but sympathize with the exasperation of citizens who were constantly being told, 'I am a fool, but at least I am not as big a fool as you are.' Nor is it ever a great intellectual achievement to display the fallacies of popular belief and the clay feet of popular idols. Anytus and his colleagues had no small ground for saying: 'We may be fools, and we are not the pets of any oracle, but at least, in our foolish way, we are trying to do something for the State—we are taking risks and making sacrifices and doing hard, thankless work. But what are you doing, except "bringing the government into hatred and contempt"? You are casting doubt on everything we do and stand for; you are undermining all the foundations of society—a cheap feat for a clever idler who boasts that he has never done anything in public life! And look at the results—Alcibiades, Critias, Plato, Xenophon—all men who have either done harm to their country or repudiated its service! These are your disciples—and by their fruits ye shall know them!'

Socrates had no real answer, and hardly attempted one; and it is a commonplace to say that he was 'justly condemned'. Democracy had asserted its right to the minimum of conformity. Yet the judgement of history is that in asserting that right Athenian democracy exhibited a weakness which was soon to prove fatal. Socrates was seventy when he was prosecuted. All his life he had been, as he boasted, the Gadfly of the People, which had only not tolerated his buzzing and stinging, but apparently had been fond and almost proud of him. That he should suddenly be regarded as dangerous, that he should have exhausted patience and good humour, meant that democracy was no longer sure of itself. It was threatened by a strong Fifth Column, and within forty years it was to fall before the Dictator of Macedon. And Socrates, its victim, was to become to all posterity one of its heroes.

Democracy, then, is entitled to keep the hemlock in a dark, locked cupboard for its nonconformists and its recalcitrants; but it is an ill day, and usually the presage of approaching doom, if it ever has to administer the cup. I find it difficult to think of any real limits on opinion and doctrine (it is, of course, otherwise with conduct) in our present society. We have had a minor Socrates in our midst for the past half-century in the person of Mr. George Bernard Shaw. I suppose there is no institution of democracy or of our social life which he has not castigated or satirized in his long and prolific career. I do not, for my part, think that he has had any great influence, outside the drama, on his generation, but I never heard that anybody suggested the hemlock for him on his seventieth birthday; on the contrary, when his hour comes, there will be many tears, flowers, and honours for him, with not a little affection and certainly unfeigned respect. Gadflies seldom sting democracy to death, for it can generally reduce the inflammation by applying a sense of humour to the affected part; if it cannot do that, and reacts violently to the prick, there is something wrong with the state of the blood. Critic and crank, however extreme, do more than add to the diversity of democracy; they are sometimes useful in showing, by their very extravagance, how impossible unanimity is among mortals even in situations where unanimity seems irresistible. The price of tolerance is inexhaustible patience. The law, which in a democracy is never independent of public opinion, can safely be trusted to enforce the minimum of conformity in conduct; but the maxim of the law that 'the thought of man is not triable' is also the maxim of democracy. It may be that when nonconformist opinion is manifestly producing a greater degree of nonconformist conduct than is compatible with the peace of society, it must be arrested at the source; but in Anglo-Saxon democracy this so rarely happens that it has no practical reality. In my own lifetime I cannot recall a single example of it in British society, though I can remember the propagation of many opinions which would be worthy of nothing but instant death in any totalitarian State; and some experience of conscientious objection in time of war has taught me that there are practically no limits to the nonconformity of opinion in our community.

FREEDOM OF DISCUSSION

It follows from what has been said that if majority opinion is to possess the quality which alone can justify its authority, discussion must be free, open, and candid. There must be an opportunity for every point of view to be put. This is the principle of free speech, which is too familiar as a constitutional and social doctrine to need discussion here. In England there is, in time of peace, only one real limitation upon it, for the legal antiquities which I have mentioned concerning sedition and blasphemy are of little practical importance. The proud and 'touchy' Englishman is exceedingly jealous of his reputation, and he maintains the most severe law of libel on earth. Many believe that it is too severe, especially that part of it which makes liability for defamation quite independent of conscious intent to traduce the person who is in fact, or who claims to be, injured. I will not enter into that controversy, except to say that the rule which is so much criticized has really sprung from the growth and extension of the newspaper press. Anything which covers so wide a field of facts and personalities as a newspaper may easily commit 'unintentional' libels, even if it exercises the utmost prudence. Our courts have taken the view that there is no reason why individuals should suffer for the lapses, however blameless, of newsprint, which is, after all, put forth for the profit of its publishers. This is a risk incidental to a dangerous trade, and everybody knows that it is a risk which can be covered by insurance. Despite the penalty of unmeritorious actions to which the rule undoubtedly gives rise, it does not seem to me to be unreasonable in itself; nor is it anything but healthy that in a democracy personal reputation should be strictly safeguarded. If freedom of discussion is once allowed to degenerate into freedom of abuse, majority opinion is not likely to emerge either clean or wise. With every diffidence which one should feel in criticiz-

ing the systems of other countries, I suggest that this
is a lesson which politics and public discussion in the
United States have not yet full taken to heart.

Sir Ernest Barker distinguishes four stages of discussion normally operative in democracy—in the party,
in the electorate, in the Cabinet, and in Parliament.
This is characteristic of British political arrangements,
though it could not be applied without qualification
to other systems. There is, for example, no exact
analogy in the United States to the English principle
of Cabinet solidarity and responsibility, and if by
'Parliament' we mean, as we should mean, both
Chambers, the relative importance of discussion in
the House of Representatives and the Senate is the
reverse of the relation between the House of Commons and the House of Lords. What matters most—
or what should matter most, if the majority principle
is valid—is discussion in the electorate. There is certainly no lack of the means of discussion nowadays.
Much public attention was concentrated recently on
the Beveridge Report. Who but an actuary could
reckon the number of media through which the subject has been discussed? When we think of the *voces
populi* to-day, we have to take into account not only
political parties and meetings, but the Parish Debating Society, the local Constitutional Club and
Reform Club, Discussion Groups in the Forces and
among civilian workers, the bar parlour, the Civil
Defence Posts, the Women's Institutes, and the Guilds,
Leagues and Fellowships which are as the sands of the
sea. All these voluntary organizations, some trivial
and some pompous, some official and some unofficial,
some ephemeral and some enduring, no doubt receive
a special stimulus from the conditions of war, but they

are also extraordinarily active in time of peace. I have said nothing of newspapers (especially Sunday newspapers) nor of the reports and manifestos issued by innumerable groups, nor of the truly astonishing output of pamphlets. This latter is, to me, one of the marvels of this war, and especially of the paper control. Not a week passes but I receive two or three, from total strangers, on every conceivable subject—I have received as many as sixteen in a single batch; and my haul must be trifling compared with that of less obscure men. Milton, thou shouldst be living at this hour!

And above all is the incalculable factor of the radio. I call it incalculable, because nobody yet knows what its effect is going to be on democracy, though we know all too well what its effect can be on Totalitaria. It has carried us far beyond the Aristotelian principle of one orator being heard by the whole people, for one orator can now be heard by the entire world. In this matter the two Anglo-Saxon democracies have taken opposite lines. Wireless is a monopoly in this country, and many think that, however well it may be controlled and with whatever genuine attempt at impartiality, it is a dangerous and undemocratic monopoly. The apology for it is that it prevents the air from becoming a babel and saves the public from what is, to many members of it, the tiresome nuisance of mixing tooth-paste and breakfast foods with music and drama. In the United States, on the other hand, there are, I believe, some seven hundred transmitting stations. The air is never silent, and many Americans are so accustomed to the disembodied voice at all hours of day and night, and in every place, from the bath to the automobile, that

E

they feel lost without it, and for them the silence of
the grave will add to the terrors of death. What is
the effect of this democratic Gift of Tongues? Apart
from popular entertainment, each enterprise offers its
listeners a great variety of current commentary, and
the commentator's art has been brought to a high
degree of skill and instruction. All is 'thought pro-
voking', but the points of view range through every
conceivable shade of opinion. Outside the serious
contributions there is always the 'lunatic fringe', and
it is unquestionable that a great deal of sheer poison
has been disseminated by the radio, though it is now
restrained by war censorship. The opportunity for the
unscrupulous or self-intoxicated demagogue is too
good to miss, and from time to time very dangerous
men of this type have arisen in America. There may
be others in the future, and they may present a grave
political problem. The effect of so many divergent
voices, each striving to outdo the others, cannot fail
to be distracting to anybody who has the patience to
listen to them. But as against this inevitable confusion
of thought, there is the great advantage that diversity
of opinion counteracts that tendency to majority auto-
suggestion to which reference has been made. For
that reason alone, if there were no others, it seems
to me that America has chosen the right and the
democratic way in this extremely important matter.
Many of us would prefer the air to be comparatively
quiet, and some of us would prefer it to be altogether
silent; but if the radio is to be admitted at all as a
medium of discussion, it is difficult to justify a State
monopoly. Freedom of speech should apply as well
to the mechanical voice as to the natural voice. There
is no need for a censorship, and there ought not to be

any question of it, for it will be supplied by the combined forces of the law and of public opinion. The films, which appeal to almost as large an audience, have managed well enough with a voluntary censorship, which is, indeed, stricter and more arbitrary than any official control would be. There is the further consideration, not unimportant to listeners, that the competition of different opinions leads to a much higher and more intelligent standard of discussion than ours. There is, in my opinion, no comparison between the technique of the American commentator and the very amateurish efforts of our 'talkers'—all, no doubt, men of distinction in their own specialities, but men who have seldom made any study of the difficult art of the microphone.

The enormous variety of expressed opinion in America makes it a baffling task to assess majority opinion, and it is well known that great surprises have happened in American politics and many prophets have been confounded. Of recent years ingenious persons have devised means of ascertaining or predicting opinion by polls, ballots, and 'cross-sections'. Some of them are said to be singularly accurate and all claim to be highly scientific. They are being imitated in this country, with what success I do not know. If these experiments serve merely to increase the circulation of newspapers, to add to the profits of commercial enterprises, or to supply sociologists with material for theories and treatises, I suppose there is no objection to them in a free country; but if they influence the actions of politicians, as they appear to do, I confess I regard them with apprehension as factors in democratic life. They are extra-constitutional, unregulated, and capricious; unless both question and answer are accurate and unambiguous, they may be a fruitful source of false or arbitrary inferences; and they are too easily posed and too lightly answered. I do not know whether the administration pays much attention to them in the United States, but we have had one example in this country which was, let us hope, sufficient warning against any repetition. The notorious and disingenuous Peace Ballot in 1935 undoubtedly had an intimidating effect at Westminster and in the constituencies, and was in no small measure responsible for the delays and hesitations of our rearmament and our foreign policy—weaknesses now loudly condemned by the very people who encouraged them. Democracy has its own natural, biological ways of developing its majority opinion, or what Mr. Lindsay, adopting the Quaker phrase, calls 'the sense of the meeting', and they are not the ways of calculating machines and statistical tables, nor yet of an artificial 'public opinion' manufactured by leading questions and hasty answers.

In the Parliamentary stage of discussion, the party system has been not only the traditional method of all democracies but a first principle of their working. It has, however, taken very different forms, and there is little analogy between its manifestations in France and in the Anglo-Saxon democracies. I think it was Mr. Churchill himself who once said that the real basis of the British party system, and its difference from Continental systems, is the fact that the House of Commons is rectangular. The theory would be plausible were it not that the House of Representatives and the Senate are circular, and they have adhered to a two-party system more rigidly than ourselves. We can draw no safe conclusions about the party system from the abnormal conditions of war; but even in peace, under the influence of 'national' governments, a good deal of vitality seems to have gone out of our party system. Its effect in Parliament is altogether disproportionate to its elaborate and costly organization in the constituencies. Old Parliamentarians seem to be agreed that it has become far more perfunctory than once it was, that the Government more and more dominates the House and meets with little effective criticism in the measures which it sponsors, and that the private member feels more and more his own insignificance. If this be true, it is a misfortune in a democracy, all the more so because in these days of delegated legislation the dominance of the Government means, in large measure, the dominance of the executive.

The objections to the party system are manifest. Why, says the mugwump, should I commit myself in advance to a programme, a 'platform', or even a philosophy? I prefer to keep my judgement free for each issue as it arises. It violates all reason and logic to be bound to support the Government when I think it is wrong, or to oppose it when I think it is right.

The objection is not easily answered, for it is constantly evident in politics that support is insincere and opposition is merely factitious. If there is no real objection to a measure or a policy, opposition must still oppose; it can never admit that the wind is taken out of its sails; and the result is sometimes mere debating sophistry, the scoring of irrelevant points, and obscuration of the essential question by side-issues. In the light of history, it is difficult to read with patience to-day the Opposition speeches of

Charles James Fox, and they ring all the more hollow for the plausibility of their rhetoric.

All this admitted, *audi alteram partem* is a fundamental law of democracy. As in law, so in politics, it is imperative that the other side should be put, even when there is no other side! That would be an empty paradox if there were not a truth, too often unperceived, lurking behind it—namely, that there always *is* another side. If we are not prepared to admit that, we must at least admit that it is never safe to assume that the other side does not exist until we have searched conscientiously for it and failed to find it. The lesson of legal experience is that the seeing eye seldom fails to discover it. Even if the party system were to be regarded merely as a dialectical instrument, it would be worth preserving. For, after all, in it, and in all the clash of opinions which go to make up democratic discussion, may we not perceive that old, irrefragable principle of thesis, antithesis, and synthesis? There seems to be no Law of Nature more constant in history and in the affairs of men; and when Fascism attempts, as it does, to create the synthesis without its preliminary processes, it is—literally—flying in the face of nature.

THE RULE OF LAW

The most important practical aspect of political equality is legal equality; for justice is the cement of society—or, as a German jurist of a now defunct school has expressed it, the aim of law is the 'harmony of wills' in society; and without an impartial and easily accessible administration of justice a democratic system is inconceivable. I know of no single institution which more sharply symbolizes the gulf between democratic and totalitarian 'ideology' than the Gestapo. When an Englishman says that he would rather die than live under the regime of a secret police, he means what he says, for he knows that if such a thing should ever happen his whole world would be changed. It is only by a great strain upon his instincts, and with a firm determination to be rid of it at the earliest possible moment, that he tolerates such an emergency measure as Regulation 18B; for he knows that the danger of such expedients, even in time of war, is not only that they may be abused, or unwisely administered, but that they secretly foster the despotic elements which are always latent in any society. England has, ere now, had her taste of the spy, the sneak, and the informer. In the merry days of Titus Oates no man could trust his neighbour, and the whole of social life was poisoned. Assuredly, Englishmen would rather die outright than fight again for breath in those green, creeping clouds of choking gas.

Absolute legal equality is as unattainable, in imperfect human institutions, as absolute political equality. So long as there are disparities in wealth, it will always be possible for the rich man to prosecute his claim, or to defend himself, with more persistence and with more abundant resources than the poor man, and in that sense 'there is one law for the rich and one for the poor'. I would, however, emphatically deny that the mere fact of poverty, regarded as a matter of 'social status', places a man at any disadvantage in our Courts, or that the mere fact of wealth, similarly regarded, confers any privilege, especially in criminal law. It can also be claimed, without complacency, that the amount of actual perversion of justice through the corruption of wealth is negligible. I would only add that few laymen realize the amount of free service which is provided by the legal profession for the necessitous.

Familiar though they are, I must restate, in their simplest terms, the three principles—which are only different aspects of the same proposition—of the Rule of Law as it is understood in England. They are: (1) that the system of justice is one and uniform throughout the country; (2) that all citizens have the right, on the one hand, of recourse to it for the redress of grievances, and are, on the other hand, equally subject to its penalties for violations of rights; and (3) that no person or class of persons is placed above or below it or is entitled to claim any special and privileged type of jurisdiction. We must not confuse this third principle with special exemptions from ordinary liability which may be accorded to certain officers in special circumstances, such as judges and magistrates, or executive subordinates, in the performance of their offices, Members of Parliament 'on the floor of the House', or Ministers and their representatives in the performance of acts of State. These are, very plainly, exceptions which merely prove the rule; and the only real exception in our law is the curious historical position of the Crown, which, in matters of civil or criminal liability 'can do no wrong'. But even this is only a partial exception, for in innumerable matters the Crown may be a litigant (though under a clumsy procedure). From the days of Bracton onwards, it has never been our doctrine that the sovereign is *legibus solutus*, but *sub Deo et sub lege*, and most of our great constitutional battles have been fought on this very issue; and to-day the greater part of the royal prerogative has become nothing more than constitutional fiction, though very useful fiction. A far greater danger in the modern State has been the constant tendency to place the executive above the law. This is an insidious disease which every democracy, while recognizing the inevitable extensions of executive action in the complex modern State, must be vigilant to keep within proper bounds. It is wholly incompatible with the democratic idea, and wherever it has gained the upper hand, it has proved disastrous. Its effect upon France, which had, in proportion to population, the largest bureaucracy in Europe with the strongest executive tradition—deliberately created by Napoleon as a prime element of his totalitarian State—was paralysing; and it was not for nothing that Germany was commonly reputed to have the most 'efficient' bureaucracy on the Continent. All totalitarianism is based upon the notion of 'efficiency' as the supreme merit of State organization. I do not agree with those who detect in our British Civil Service—a body of able, conscientious, and, on the whole, just men—a constant, sinister conspiracy to seize illicit power. That is not the real point—which is, in my belief, that it is the very law of bureaucracy's being that it should strive to do things in its own 'efficient' way with the minimum of legal restraint, and that it therefore constantly seeks, often in spite of itself, to dispense itself from the law. If Parliamentary government means anything in our democracy, and if open responsibility and the representative principle mean anything, this is a grave threat to the whole democratic idea. It is highly necessary that the public should realize that there are now about a million servants of Government in this country. If the population over the age of twenty-one is, as an expert informs me, about twenty-four and a half million, this seems to mean that nearly one person in every twenty is a civil servant of some degree or other. This is not solely the result of abnormal conditions, for it is only an intensification of a process which has been going on for more than a century; and if it continues to the point where we shall all be taking in each other's washing, not much of the Rule of Law will be left.

Far above and beyond the practical applications of the Rule of Law there is a principle of the utmost moment not only to democracy, but to the whole of humanity—namely, that justice is an end in itself, and must be pursued unflinchingly, whatever the inconveniences to individuals or to governments. The contrary principle, which is established in all totalitarian societies, is that justice is an instrument of policy. To any true democrat, this is the ultimate and unpardonable heresy, the sin against the light. Law, thus interpreted, is power; and the whole meaning of the Rule of Law is that it is restraint on power. In the *Law Quarterly Review* for April 1943 there appears a remarkable article by an anonymous writer, apparently of German nationality. I cannot do better than quote his eloquent words:

'The Rule of Law puts political power at a discount. It checks the ambitious politician in his fight for power and in his use of power. The more unscrupulous and adventurous he is, the more noticeable is the check. The Rule of Law not only bars some ways of obtaining power, it limits access to it to certain more or less strictly defined avenues of approach. By prescribing conditions, forms, terms and limits of its use, it diminishes the chances connected with the holding of power in general. No quick success remedies the faults by which the success has been obtained. Only time may remedy them. Law balances the various social forces in a nation which are fighting for supremacy. Their fight is a natural, not an obnoxious thing. It is an expression of life and vigour. The Rule of Law does not prevent the fight, or at least a good one does not attempt to do so. It only provides rules of combat and regulations for defining the winner. It prevents the fight from becoming continuous and protects the defeated party from being crushed. It tries to distribute the spoils of victory in a fair way and to maintain the unity of the State and nation in spite of the conflicting aims of different groups.'

Democracy can never afford to lose sight of these principles. For my part, I do not think it can afford to do so even in time of war and in the face of gigantic perils. The patriotic judge is to be feared even more than the patriotic administrator. Not long ago, purely on a question of legal interpretation, a number of detainees were released in India, to the great embarrassment of the Government in a very anxious situation. To me, this is a more admirable spectacle of democracy than the 1,700 persons in England who, in the name of security, have been detained for indefinite periods without trial, indictment, or hope of redress. The quality of the Just Judge is that of the Happy Warrior, who

> through the heat of conflict, keeps the law
> In calmness made, and sees what he foresaw.

LIBERTY OF THE INDIVIDUAL

Heart and pen quail as they approach this subject. Is there anything new to be said about it? Certainly a writer untrained in philosophical method can hope to add little to a problem which has caused all the wisest heads among humanity to ache throughout the ages. I approach it, therefore, with the utmost diffidence; but, with the desperation of diffidence, I will at once make bold to assert what seems to me the only possible 'aim of government'. It is formulated by John Stuart Mill, after examination of some of the other aims which have been commonly attributed to government (such as order, utility, and happiness), and it is expressed in language which any man can understand.

'If we ask ourselves on what causes and conditions good government in all its senses, from the humblest to the most exalted, depends, we find that the principal of them, the one which transcends all others, is the qualities of the human beings composing the society over which the government is exercised.' (*Representative Government*, ch. II.)

The two aspects of government, Mill insists, are its effect upon men and upon things, 'what it makes of the citizens and what it does with them'. And this is a principle which goes far beyond mere politics—it involves an interpretation of the whole of life and the part which man must play in it. I will borrow again from Mill; and there is a certain irony, not without sadness, in the fact that the words which I am about to quote come from a member of that nation which now spits upon them. He was Wilhelm von Humboldt, and Mill quotes thus from him:

' "The end of man, or that which is prescribed by the eternal or immutable dictates of reason, and not suggested by vague and transient desires, is the highest and most harmonious development of his powers to a complete and consistent whole". The object "towards which every human being must ceaselessly direct his efforts, and on which especially those who design to influence their fellow men must ever keep their eyes, is the individuality of power and development"; for this there are two requisites, "freedom, and variety of situations"; and from the union of these arise "individual vigour and manifold diversity", which combine themselves in "originality".' (*On Liberty*, ch. III.)

In short, the law of life goes beyond the Oracle's injunction to Know Thyself (though that is the first commandment) and bids thee Realize Thyself. 'Become what thou art!' cried Zarathustra. And the Good Life at which the State should aim is the life in which this self-development can find the freest scope, consistently with the self-development of others.

The man of faith looks to a divine pattern as his guide. Being, as he believes, made in the image of God, he seeks to bring the image ever nearer to the model. The materialist cries, with Swinburne:

> A creed is a rod,
> And a crown is of night;
> But this thing is God,
> To be man with thy might,
> To grow straight in the strength of thy spirit,
>   and live out thy life as the light.

The materialist believes that the man of faith seeks artificial and delusive support in his supreme human task. The man of faith believes that the materialist is, in spite of himself, performing an act of faith which must be founded in something greater than himself. Both are agreed that true self-development is progression not to mere power or strength (as the hero-worshipper believes), but to the good and the right; for, whether in theological doctrine or in social philosophy, the highest faculties of man cannot lead to any other end. 'The human good', said Aristotle, 'is an energy of the spirit according to special capacity, and if there are several such capacities, then according to the best and fullest of them, *but always in a full life.*' Has anybody ever better expressed a code of conduct for the self-respecting man? The Good Life, despite the delusion of ascetics, cannot be good without being full; and democratic diversity is one aspect of the full life. There is still dignity and inspiration for suffering men in the old Stoic ideal of equilibrium attained through strife.

When all is said, what other possible object can there be for government or social systems or New Orders or Old Orders, or for all the -isms, except the individual, who alone is capable of *living*? Mussolini has written: 'All is in the State, and nothing that is human or spiritual exists, far less has value, apart from the State. In that sense Fascism is totalitarian, and the Fascist State, the synthesis and unity of all values, interprets and develops and energizes *all* the life of the people.' Wild and whirling words, my lord; for what can they mean when translated into reality? How can the State live and die, and laugh and grieve, and love and hate, and feel all the emotions and thoughts and experiences which make up the only life that is known to humanity? Can Leviathan live in a cottage and bring up a family? In what manner, save that of rhetoric and metaphor, can it be the 'synthesis of all values'? Values exist for human beings and only human beings can assess them, because they alone can *feel* them. We are again in the presence of the old anthropomorphic fallacy. What this word-spinner is really picturing is a gigantic omniscient, omnicompetent *man*; and the State is not a man, but an abstraction. It is the same fallacy which leads men to believe that because an aggregate of persons has undoubtedly an identity of its own, it is a 'real personality'—by which they only mean that it is a real, aggregate *man*. This is to become the dupe of figures of speech, as was done most conspicuously by the early sociologists who thought of society as an 'organism' with limbs and organs and faculties and bio-chemical metabolism.

There is no unit of existence except the individual, and for him, and by him and through him, all systems of government exist. Even totalitarian systems really exist for him, though they pretend otherwise; and this is a fact which we are too apt to forget. We constantly say that the effect of Fascist regimentation is to 'destroy individuality', but we err if we imagine that, in its first manifestations, it necessarily saps the vitality of the individual. There is such a thing as finding yourself by losing yourself. Millions of men have had that experience in military organization. It is a frequent claim of the anti-militarist that the soldier becomes a mere mindless, will-less automaton. I do not think that that is the experience of the normal man. There is something extraordinarily exhilarating in being a part, to the utmost of one's capacity, of a huge, concerted effort far beyond one's own individual powers, in an objective sphere which is often a refreshing contrast to the pettiness of personal, subjective concerns. It is a profound mistake to suppose that the soldier who is part of a well-executed drill-movement is behaving like a mechanical toy. He is at full stretch, he is making exacting demands on himself, and he is deriving something galvanic from the sense of co-operation. The soldier who is slack on parade is not usually an individualist rebelling against being a robot, but a man of weak individuality and defective will. No normal person who has ever taken part in a ceremonial parade can have failed to feel its electrical and strangely emotional quality. The present writer has never met any human creature whom he was more anxious to please than the Guards sergeant-major who once drilled him, nor anybody who ever extracted from him more intense, willing, and pleasurable effort. Nor can there be any normal person who, being engaged in a total war, has not felt himself vitalized, expanded, and even ennobled by the immensity of the corporate activity in which he is engaged. Were it not for this tremendous compensating factor, who would endure without faltering the hardships, perils, and brutalities of modern war? It is, indeed, one of the problems of civilization that nothing which peace has yet devised can quite replace the incomparable stimulus of the life-and-death contest, and, until it has done so, it seems only too probable that man, being an animal, will continue to turn, even against his will, to this supreme test of animal vitality.

Multiply this influence a thousandfold, carry it into every relationship of public and private life, implant it in infancy and foster it throughout adolescence, beat it into the brain by every means of suggestion and exhortation, and the passion of 'corporateness' easily becomes a powerful drug which we should be foolish to underestimate. But the penalty is manifest. Man cannot live on drugs, and the dose must be constantly increased to produce its effect; and then comes the time when it fails altogether, and nothing is left but a paralysed will and a shattered constitution. The soldier's sense of collective vitality and concentrated effort is a valuable experience in life; but few men would or could live all their lives at battle-pitch, and, indeed, it is common observation that those who cannot summon up their best energies except under that extreme urge are often ineffectual or even amoral in the ordinary relations of life. We must relax from intensity; we cannot live perpetually on 'heights that the soul is competent to gain', there cannot be exaltation without repose. But the mania of the State can never relax; it is power, and power must ever drive and command even when it is pretending to cajole. The State-worshipper comes to the altar with uplifted hands and shining eyes, and soon his hands are nerveless and his eyes are blind, and the evil spirits that haunt it make the very temple itself a prison-house. Obedience, to possess any virtue, must be the act of a free-willing creature; unreasoning obedience to a Fuehrer who is superhuman, or to a Duce who is 'always right', is Nietzsche's slave-morality indeed. Thus an impulse which began as a strong and natural stimulus to individuality becomes the negation of all individuality; men in this condition, being themselves dehumanized, are the potential enemies of all that gives humanity its savour, its variety, and its loving-kindness.

If self-culture, or the development of individuality is a human good, it follows that liberty is a human good, because liberty is the condition of that development. Every creature, then, should enjoy the maximum of liberty; but to say that is merely to pose a conundrum, since the eternal problem of all govern-

F

ment is, what is the due proportion between the liberty of each and the liberty of all? How can one man enjoy freedom without subtracting from the freedom of another, and how much should each surrender to the other in order to create the Greatest Common Measure for the totality?

In one form or another, this is the Sphinx riddle which runs through all political theory. It is the origin of all the false analogies of the Social Contract fantasy, which attempted to find, in an actual binding agreement among men, constitutional authority either for their mutual surrender of liberty *inter se* or its surrender to an appointed sovereign. The riddle appears repeatedly in legal theory, and receives precisely opposite answers from different theorists. Some tell us that the object of all legal rules is to enlarge liberty, others that every legal rule is necessarily a fetter on liberty. The latter view was epitomized in Tom Paine's 'all government is a necessary evil', which is to say that every act of social regulation is an abridgement of the absolute good of individual liberty; and this in its turn seems to mean (as some indeed hold) that anarchy would be the true state of blessedness, were men only good enough for it. Another legal form of the riddle centres in the conception of rights and duties. Does law exist primarily to confer rights—i.e. attributions of power, according to one school of thought, or delimitations of interest, according to another—or to impose duties, i.e. to restrain liberty in relation either to other individuals or to the State? The Positivist school of Comte insisted that the individual in society possessed only duties, and no rights whatsoever except 'the right to do his duty' (whatever that may mean). The theological analogue is the grim Calvinistic canon that 'all that is not duty is sin'. In recent years this doctrine has been powerfully expounded by a French jurist, Léon Duguit, whose theories have undoubtedly exercised much influence in building up Fascist jurisprudence. Another form of the riddle concerns the function of the State itself. Does it exist in order to make demands on the individual, and so curtail his 'natural' freedom of action, or does it exist, as Dr. Bosanquet says, to 'hinder hindrances' to the good life, and so perpetually afford the individual better opportunities for self-development? It is pleasing, and a little romantic, to think of the State as the 'hinderer of hindrances', but nowadays the State is a great deal more than that. It no longer confines itself to the negative function of removing burdens, it is constantly engaged in conferring benefits. It does not merely sweep obstacles from the path, it marks out the path and guides the individual's footsteps along it, as the Prime Minister has told us, 'from the cradle to the grave'. Consider, for example, the change which has come over the theory of legislation. In the sixteenth century, our Courts were able to lay it down that the object of a statute was to 'remedy a mischief', and the principle of judicial interpretation was therefore simple—the judge must inquire what was the mischief aimed at and what remedy the legislature had ordained; he could then apply the remedy in accordance with the legislature's intent. Nobody to-day imagines that statutory interpretation is as simple as all that. It has not been as simple as all that since the coming of Jeremy Bentham. A whole history of 'social policy' often lies behind the enactments which judges are daily called on to administer, and their task would be vastly simplified if they could fall back on straightforward tests of mischiefs and remedies, hindrances and emancipations. As it is, unkind critics sometimes reproach them because they are not sociologists, psychologists, economists, and philosophers, as well as legal interpreters.

When so many others have failed, it is a forlorn hope to try to answer the Sphinx; but it seems to me that a great deal must depend on whether we regard liberty as an absolute or a relative quantity in itself. I find it difficult to grasp the conception either of 'natural' liberty or 'natural' right. Man being a social animal, both liberty and right exist, and can only exist, by social relationship. 'Man is born free, and is everywhere in chains.' In what sense is he born free? There are chains upon him from the moment of his birth—chains of heredity and environment and association with other human beings. At no stage of his existence can he rid himself of those gyves. No man is completely free so long as there is any other man on earth. It is meaningless to say that a man on a desert island is completely free. Apart from the facts that this is a quite abnormal situation of mankind, and that nearly every desert island has its Man Friday, who immediately raises questions of right and duty, and that there is generally a ship on the horizon which links the hermit to the rest of the world—apart from these practical considerations, there is no liberty unless there is at least the possibility of restraint, and the desert island, if it is truly 'desert', excludes, by hypothesis, even the contingency of restraint. If we take a more extreme example, and imagine a man as the sole survivor on earth of the human race, how can there be, in such a situation, any question of liberty or bondage, of right or of duty? Liberty and right are not segments carved from areas naturally boundless; they are the circumferences of intersecting circles within the greater circles of society and humanity.

All liberty being relative, it is misleading to conceive the State as either diminishing or amplifying the individual's sphere of 'natural' liberty, and it begs the question to assume that the starting-point of State action is either the vindication of rights or the imposition of duties. It is neither, or both—it really matters not, in practice, which view we take. The State, in 'civilized' communities, is the agency set up to adjust and define the relative spheres of liberty and right. But the State does not thereby create artificial out of 'natural' liberty, nor is it the only instrumentality which can make the adjustments. Long before the modern state was dreamt of, men had found those adjustments for themselves, and no society would have been for a moment possible without them. There is no greater fallacy in the Hobbesian allegory than the notion that the 'natural' condition of any aggregate of 'natural' men is free-for-all internecine strife. This is not the condition even of beasts; there is a law of the pack, and of the hive and of the jungle. All creatures of like kind associate together instinctively by herd discipline; man is the only animal who deliberately seeks to destroy his own species. It is, again, a common error romantically to picture the primitive life as simple. The life of primitive peoples is extremely complex. It is hemmed in at all points by elaborate rules of observance and superstition affecting not only the living but the dead. Rights and duties are intricately distributed and far more rigorously enforced than among advanced nations. Massive brows have been wrinkled by the degrees of affinity which govern endogamic and exogamic marriages—a labyrinth to which the only analogy that occurs to the mind is our modern Emergency Regulations. Among such peoples or among a far higher type like an Arabian tribe, the civilized man commits a fault of social deportment with almost every word and movement. No State has drawn upon a blackboard all these intersecting circles; men have found them, and continue to maintain them, by the mysterious processes of custom and tradition. When, at a far later stage of development, the State either replaces the more indefinite forces of cohesion; or, as it is probably more true to say, when the State is added to the others as the dominant instrument of cohesion; it is merely continuing and making more explicit the process of adjustment which has always been inherent in the very nature of society. Its law always strives to be the 'harmony of wills'. In short, the natural condition of men is not natural liberty, but a natural compromise of liberty, and the exact terms of that compromise are an exceedingly delicate problem in any society, primitive or civilized.

No law, no mathematical proportions, can be formulated for it; and the attempt at a formula seems to be not only fruitless but mischievous. Mill's principle was that 'to individuality should belong the part of life in which it is chiefly the individual that is interested; to society, the part which chiefly interests society'. But Mill failed to answer, though he noticed, the objection which the moralist immediately makes —that it is impossible to draw a distinct line between these two spheres. Anything which interests the individual in the long run interests society. A man's 'private life' is seldom wholly private. Nobody can be an entirely depraved individual without becoming, sooner or later, at least a nuisance, and probably a danger, to others. It needs no theological doctrine of sin, nor any high exposition of ethics, to teach a man of ordinary reason and self-control that in his social life good character, like honesty, is 'the best policy'. It is therefore a perpetual problem of social regulation how far law should attempt to control private morals or to enforce what are (fallaciously, as I believe) called self-regarding duties. It is, for example, a debatable question in our law why suicide should be a crime, or why homosexuality should be *per se* an offence, when other forms of indecency, not involving public scandal, are not so treated. Mill himself, in several illustrations, showed how impalpable is the line between private and public interest. In his day, millions of people believed, and believed fiercely, that a husband's control over the person and property of his wife, and a father's control over the education of his children, were essentially matters which concerned the individual and nobody else. Mill protested vehemently against these popular dogmas, holding that these were eminently matters which concerned the State. Everybody knows that his opinion prevailed, and that within a generation the State asserted authority in both these spheres—though not without violent protests about the invasion of personal liberty.

While it is impossible to lay down a rigid line of demarcation, it is not difficult to find examples of circumstances in which democratic sentiment instinctively demands liberty of choice for the individual. It is still an offence, punishable by ecclesiastical censures, for a member of the Church of England not to attend his parish church on Sunday. Such is the law, as it results from a long and complicated course of legislation, but if anybody attempted to enforce it, every reasonable man would arise and smite it. After centuries of agony and shame, we have learned that religious conviction and practice are now solely the affair of the individual; and the number of different forms of worship and belief now existing in this country are quite past counting or credence. The Church of God, the Only Church of God, and the Only True Church of God, all, in their several conventicles, are recognized as being nobody's affair but their own. Again, in matters of sex, we have never gone to the zealot's extreme of logic—for the extreme of logic is always unwisdom—in holding that all matters of private morality are matters of public concern; but there are nowadays a number of statues which protect the young against exploitation by the libertine, and nobody thinks them unwise or unnecessary.

One of the test cases of liberty which has been before the public for many years is that of intoxicating liquor. There can be no question that alcohol has wrought great havoc in society, though the damage has enormously diminished in recent years. The Prohibitionist says that if you suppress this easy means of degeneration, you have removed a danger so threatening to the community that any deprivation which may be caused to moderate persons is vastly outweighed. It is not a sufficient answer to him to say that everything is capable of abuse, because some things are obviously more capable of abuse than others. Nor is it an entirely convincing answer to say that every individual, for his own soul's sake, must be left to resist temptation by the strength of his own will. Every civilized system of law recognizes a duty to protect the weak, in some circumstances, against themselves. I can imagine some situations in which it might be necessary, in the general interest, to suppress certain forms of strong drink; for example, it is said that absinthe was forbidden in France because addiction to it had a sterilizing effect which accentuated gravely the already serious problem of declining birth-rate. Nobody, surely, would hesitate to proscribe the noxious fluid known as Red Biddy, the sole object of which is rapid and violent intoxication. Or consider, again, the matter of narcotic drugs. I do not recollect whether Herbert Spencer ever referred to the subject, but I can imagine him saying that if a man desired to ruin his body and soul with heroin, that was entirely his own responsibility before God and man. It is possible, I believe, to indulge 'moderately' in drugs—indeed, there is a strong case for saying that the normal individual can hardly support existence without stimulants of some kind. The history of tobacco is astonishing; from very early times it has been prized and demanded by men of all stages of civilization, and it has survived all the attempts (often Draconic) of kings, sultans and popes to suppress it. Enormous quantities of tea, coffee, and tobacco are consumed, and I would make bold to say that it would be impossible for the British nation to fight this war without tea and tobacco, which are munitions of prime importance. But men, and women even more, have been known to damage their digestions—and perhaps their characters!—with strong tea; Dr. Johnson recognized it as a vice, but impenitently gloried in it. Tobacco has added substantially to the revenues of the medical profession. Balzac practically killed himself with coffee, and Edgar Wallace—I apologize for the collocation—with sweet tea. On the other hand, I

have known an old man, very well-preserved in body
and mind, who for many years of his life had taken
large quantities of laudanum; I believe that life-long
moderate indulgence in opium is common among the
Chinese; and one of the finest lecturers and scholars I
ever encountered (he died at a great age, full of
honours) for a good fifty years of his life never drank
less than a bottle of whisky a day and was often visibly
'affected' in the performance of his academic duties.
Amid all these vagaries of tolerance or intolerance of
poisons, on what principle of public interest and private liberty are we to say that alcohol and tobacco
should be permitted and cocaine prohibited? I think
that we can say no more than this, that alcohol is a
substance which, properly used, can give great pleasure and do little harm; that the average man can and
does use it reasonably and that it is unjust and disproportionate to deprive him of that pleasure for the
sake of persons who are not of average control. Narcotic drugs, on the other hand, cannot give pleasure
without disproportionate danger; the average person
cannot become habituated to them without physical
and mental demoralization, and it is not unjust, in the
interest of the average, to deprive the exceptional few
of drugs for which they have a peculiar tolerance.
Similarly, for one victim of nicotine poisoning there
are ten thousand smokers who derive help and satis-
faction from their drug, and it would be monstrous to
deprive them of their legitimate indulgence—though
the attempt has been made, and there are still States
in America where it is illegal to sell cigarettes. If the
all too obvious propositions which I have been ad-
vancing are doubted, the appeal to experience should
convince. The American democracy allowed itself to

be jockeyed into the experiment of prohibition, and it is unnecessary, at this time of day, to dilate on the results of the experiment. Go beyond the reasonab'e controls of personal liberty, and the reactions of excess, depredation, and disrepute of law are truly appalling. There is a savage part of man which, when under the censorship of decent social behaviour, can hold itself in check, but, when caged and whipped, becomes a roaring beast. A little too much law, and you turn the moderate drinker into a dipsomaniac, the agnostic into a blasphemer, the enlightened employer into a Gradgrind, and the flirt into a harlot.

Another 'social evil' of which we hear a great deal is gambling. I leave aside that aspect of it which is considered by some to be a moral problem, because I can see no morals in it. The proposition that it is morally wrong to 'get something for nothing', or to 'enjoy the fruits of labour without the labour', is, to me, so manifestly contrary to experience of life with all its accidents of fortune, that I would as soon call it a sin to accept a legacy. The only moral problem, as in the case of alcohol, is one of moderation or excess; and I can see no possible reason for legal restraint on gambling except restraint on unscrupulous exploitation of the public. But that is not the principle on which our betting laws are based. The gaming-house, it is true, is illegal, because highly likely to be fraudulent. But the notorious football pools—said to represent the largest single volume of betting money in the country—resist all threats of legislation. The street bookmaker is interdicted, but the bookmaker in the luxurious offices of a limited company plies and advertises his trade unhindered. The worst feature of this charivari is not its wickedness but its inconsistency.

I do not understand on what principle it can be right to gamble in private and wrong to gamble in a 'public place' (other than a racecourse!). There is no analogy with public and private indecency, because it is impossible to say that the spectacle of two men tossing pennies in the street scandalizes the public. The truth is that we, as a nation, do not know, or will not determine, what our real morality is on this question. The Puritan tradition frowns on gambling as a worldly vanity, while the average Englishman more instinctively inclines to gambling than anybody else in Europe. Our laws on the subject are consequently a deplorable muddle; and the result is that a raffle is a crime and the Derby is a national festival. If there is any justice in the charge of hypocrisy which is so often levelled at us, here, certainly, is support for it. And it must be added, in sorrow, that there is no worse example in our society of 'one law for the rich and one for the poor'.

In matters of hygiene, we have already reached a point which must cause convulsions to the spirit of Herbert Spencer, who once said, I believe, that it was better that the community should be afflicted with smallpox than that a single individual should be compulsorily vaccinated. We can no longer accept the principle, upon which Mill, not long before the great Public Health Act of 1875, was silent, that his own health is essentially a matter for the individual, for science has taught us that it may be of immense importance to other individuals. Under the urgency of war, we have accepted it as a painful social necessity that a woman may be required, under penalty, to submit to medical examination for infectious disease. Enormous problems remain, the greatest being the eugenic aspect of marriage. Every democratic instinct revolts against the notion of making marriage subject to medical censorship, but if race-survival is threatened, this may some day be necessary. Certainly it is difficult, in a community with a declining population, to justify the unrestrained propagation of mental defectives, and not even a Spencer could regard a Jukes Family as a very admirable democratic institution. Is the day coming when we shall all be compelled by law to consume so many units of proteids, carbohydrates, and vitamins per day? I vaguely remember one of Mr. H. G. Wells's stories of the future in which a convivial meal consisted of various courses of grey pellets and blue jellies. So far as I can understand, hardly any section of humanity eats what is really good for it, and most eat what is definitely bad for them. If Bentham had had the scientific data at his disposal, he would have had no hesitation in prescribing nourishment by legislation; and, indeed, any expert could prescribe a diet for a far more eupeptic race than now inhabits the globe. Japan, I believe, has put its entire population on a scientific diet. I hope we may still regard pellets and jellies and syrups as totalitarian horrors, and, while learning from our doctors, and from our own common sense, to eat and drink more intelligently than our fathers and grandfathers did, to retain liberty sometimes to give ourselves indigestion. Indigestion has been a great spur to effort in human history and perfect health has seldom produced the greatest works of mind and imagination. Progress is not to be expected from a nation of prizefighters, and Sparta, with her worship of physical fitness, has not lived as long in history as Athens, which placed physical prowess in proper proportion to creative imagination.

While we have admitted all these restraints, unthinkable but a short time ago, on personal liberty, we have maintained a far greater latitude for conscience than any other country in the world. In the face of the greatest threat which has ever been offered to our existence, and despite the pressing need of man-power, we have exempted on grounds of conscience over sixty thousand persons from military service, and every kind of objection—religious, ethical, economic, and political—is admitted by the tribunals if established by satisfactory evidence.

If there is any truth in Emerson's aphorism about consistency, then, verily, we are a great-minded people in our inconsistency. I am not criticizing this —I merely note it as an interesting example of our attitude towards personal liberty in which it is indeed difficult to be consistent and dangerous to be rigid. But I would add that the word 'conscience' is sometimes put to strange uses in our society. I do not understand how anybody can have a 'conscientious' objection to being vaccinated. This is not a matter of ethics at all; there may be a scientific or merely personal objection to physical inoculation, and it may be worth while recognizing it; but it cannot be a moral issue. Again I do not criticize, but cite this only as an example of our sensitiveness to anything which describes itself as conscience, even when it seems to amount to little more than vagary.

I turn again to the law for an example of what seems to me a reasonable restraint on individual action, with a reasonable margin left for individual judgement. *Caveat emptor* is an ancient maxim of our law. But it does not mean, and it never has meant (not even in its Roman origins), that any rogue can take advantage of any fool. The maxim is modified by a great many exceptions concerning express and implied warranties, and, like every other contract, sale is always subject to rules about fraud and innocent misrepresentation. In this respect our law takes a shrewd and rather unexpected view. It says that the best way to deal with a cheat is to catch him in his own noose. His victim therefore has the option of saying either: 'The basis of the bargain is gone, and the whole deal is off, and what is more, if your misrepresentation was deliberate, I will have damages from you'; or he can say: 'You tried to cheat me, but I find that the bargain is profitable after all, and I hold you to it.' The cheat is never allowed to reply: 'Owing to my own misrepresentation, this bargain is not a bargain at all, because we were never at one about it, and you shall have no profit by it and no action upon it.'

With these limitations, persons in negotiation must exercise their own judgements, and it is never a ground for repudiation that a person of normal capacity, with fair opportunities of inspection and appraisal, has got the worst of a bargain. The seller who simply says: 'There are the goods—take them or leave them' is safe, even if he is guilty of the 'moral' fraud that he knows of a defect which it may require considerable shrewdness to discover. It is settled, for example, that 'there is no law against selling (or letting) a tumble-down house'. A house may contain a great many defects which it is difficult to discern, but it is for the purchaser or tenant to discover them. On the other hand, it is not permissible to let, for immediate occupation, a furnished house which is unfit for human habitation, because all reasonable persons realize, without expressly saying so, that in that event the whole arrangement is meaningless and worthless.

Contrast with these sensible rules, based on age-long experience of men and their dealings, some of our Emergency Regulations. One of them makes it a criminal offence to sell a stick of rhubarb with more than a specified amount of leaf upon it. I will assume, though I do not really believe it, that in war conditions it is necessary, in this fantastic manner, to guard the poor purchaser against the chicanery of the Machiavellian rhubarb-merchant. But any such provision in time of peace would be, I suggest, wasteful and ridiculous excess in protection of the purchaser. Any housewife in possession of her faculties would say: 'I will not pay the price of rhubarb for rhubarb-leaf, and I am going next door where the greengrocer will give me honest dealing.' Unless we are to imagine, as I hope we need not, a vast and nation-wide conspiracy among greengrocers, the natural laws of competition, not to mention the decent honesty of the average trader, will look after a matter of this kind. Let anybody study the Departmental definition of a Grade I egg or a seedling onion and ask himself what the condition of daily dealings would be if these 'controls' were exercised in peace-time, as many doctrinaires hope that they will be and some deliberately design that they shall be. The democratic State is not, as the Almighty Himself was once described, a *procurator fatuorum*.

It may well be objected here that I am assembling merely a collection of contradictions which contrast unfavourably with the rectilinear arrangements of the Fascist State. Let it be granted; but there is room in democracy even for contradictions. It has already been said that it is impossible to define with precision the spheres of personal liberty and collective control, and it has been implied that the demarcation of those spheres may and does vary from age to age. Continental jurists have written much about a 'natural law with variable content', the content fluctuating with the time and circumstances of different periods; and that time-spirit must be left to find and prescribe the appropriate balance between the vitality of the part and the homogeneity of the whole. Its solution will depend upon the temperament and tradition of a particular people. Tocqueville[1] wrote long ago:

'There are nations which have tirelessly pursued freedom through every kind of peril and hardship. They loved it, not for its material benefits; they regarded freedom itself as a gift so precious and so necessary that no other could console them for the loss of that which consoles them for the loss of everything else. . . . I attempt no analysis of that great emotion for those who cannot feel it. It enters of its own accord into the generous hearts which God has prepared to receive it; it fills them, it inspires them; but to the meaner minds which have never felt it, it is past finding out.'

Our whole history shows that we have been among the nations which Tocqueville describes, and that our spirit has not been without its influence in the world. But while we can never relinquish the principle, either for ourselves or for humanity at large, that government is not justified in usurping the whole province of personal liberty of action, we must not demand that all nations shall interpret the relation-

---

[1] Quoted by Mr. David Thomson, *The Democratic Ideal in France and England*.

G

ship between State and individual in the same manner
as ourselves. No more than we desire uniformity
among individuals should we desire uniformity
among governments. We must hear with respect the
opinion of Dr. Salazar, the Dictator of Portugal, when
he says (*Doctrine and Action*) that 'one of the greatest
fallacies of the nineteenth century was that English
parliamentarism and English democracy were adapt-
able to every European country'; for we have never
regarded our democracy as a commodity for export,
except within our own Empire, and even there with
many variations. It is impossible to read the opinions
of Dr. Salazar, head of a 'Government of Professors',
without feeling that he is essentially what we should
call in England a liberal-minded man. Nothing seems
to be farther from his temperament than power for
power's sake, and his conception of the State is poles
apart from the Nazi or the Bolshevik Leviathan, both
of which he fears and repudiates. Yet he is the incum-
bent of what he himself calls a 'Dictatorship of Reason
and Intelligence'—a Dictatorship none the less—and
Englishmen swallow hard when they read in his pages:
'We are anti-parliamentarians, anti-democrats, anti-
liberals, and we are determined to establish a cor-
porative State.' Lest we be too dogmatic and too self-
satisfied in our theories of democratic liberty, let us
hear this remarkable man, whose sincerity and whose
perspicacity are equally unquestionable, on that subject:

'We learn through our reason and experience that
it is not possible to erect on this idea of liberty a political system which will properly guarantee individual
and collective liberties, although with some reason
one has in the name of liberty been able to defend all

forms of oppression and arbitrary rule. We have also seen how the people were flattered by the expression "sovereignty of the people"; yet it did not give them, as a national group, either influence in the march of public affairs or that which they had most need of, whether they were sovereign or not, which was to be well governed. We have seen the extent to which the virtues of equality and the advantages of democracy have been disseminated, and how fraternity meant a descent to the lowest levels of society; this in spite of the natural inequalities and of the different grades and values which exist in all ordered societies.

'What we want, then, is to be more positive, more sincere, in our policy.

'Let us then invest the State with the necessary force in order that it may keep order, without which society cannot exist and prosper. Let us organize its powers so that it may function normally without plots and revolutions. Let us permit the State the extension of its activities, except in such cases where they might endanger the harmony of our social life. Let us define the duties and guarantees of individuals and communities, and let us also defend these ideals in such a way that the State shall not be indifferent to our rights and the citizen shall not fail in his duties. This is liberty.'

Throughout Dr. Salazar's thought runs the same 'realist' policy. His argument is that in the particular circumstances of Portugal, the choice is between anarchy and misery on the one hand and authority and well-being on the other; and that in the political conditions of that nation it is nonsense to pretend, in the name of liberty, 'that the administration of the law can be carried out by the mob instead of by an *élite* whose duty it is to lead and to sacrifice itself for the rest of the community.'

It is not for one nation to judge the political exigencies and preferences of another; but the greatest respect which we can feel for a sincere patriot like Dr. Salazar cannot prevent us from asking certain questions which he never attempts to answer. Has not every tyrant justified himself by the necessity of 'strong' government to repress anarchy?

> Thus spake the Fiend, and with Necessity,
> The tyrant's plea, excused his devilish deeds.

Who elects the *élite*, and what is to prevent their title to rule being sheer superiority of cunning or of might? What are the limits of authority? If it is necessary, for the sake of order, to suppress the dissent of the Malignants, what guarantee is there that the reasonable dissent of Benignants will not also be suppressed? What government yet devised by man is really fit to decide in all circumstances, of its own omniscience, what is best for a people? And, above all, how can irresponsible power be prevented from feeding upon itself— how can authority, even if it begins with the most benevolent intentions, be restrained from the vice of all autocracy, which is to regard its own survival as the supreme consideration? All history shows that a monopoly of right is destined, of its very nature, to become a monopoly of wrong.

These, then, seem to be some of the elements of social and individual life which democracy strives to maintain and which it believes promote the Good Life. Is it possible to describe the Good Life? I said previously that there is little analogy between ancient

and modern democracy; but for a description of the
'democratic way of life' I am going back to Athens
and to words borrowed from one of the greatest
utterances of literature. Pericles told his fellow-
citizens, assembled to do honour to their valiant
dead:[1]

'We live under a form of government which does
not emulate the institutions of our neighbours; on the
contrary, we are ourselves a model which some follow,
rather than the imitators of other peoples. It is true
that our government is called a democracy, because
its administration is in the hands, not of the few, but
of the many; yet while, in respect of law, all men are
on an equality for the settlement of their private dis-
putes, in respect of the value set on them it is as each
man is in any way distinguished that he is preferred
to public honours, not because he belongs to a particular class, but because of personal merits; nor,
again, on the ground of poverty is a man barred from
a public career by obscurity of rank if he but has it in
him to do the State a service. And not only in our public life are we liberal, but also in our freedom from
suspicion of one another in the pursuits of everyday
life; for we do not feel resentment at our neighbour if
he does as he likes, nor yet do we put on sour looks
which, though harmless, are painful to behold. But
while we thus avoid giving offence in our private
intercourse, in our public life we are restrained from
lawlessness chiefly through reverent fear, for we ren-
der obedience to those in authority and to the laws,
and especially to those laws which are ordained for the
succour of the oppressed and those which, though un-

[1] C. Forster Smith's translation (Loeb Classics), with some
minor variants.

written, bring upon the transgressor a disgrace which all men recognize.

'Moreover, we have provided for the spirit many relaxations from toil: we have games and sacrifices regularly throughout the year and homes fitted out with good taste and elegance; and the delight we find each day in these things drives away sadness. And our city is so great that all the products of all the earth flow in upon us, and ours is the happy lot to gather in the good fruits of our own soil with no more home-felt security of enjoyment than we do those of other lands.'

Let it be remembered that this is a picture of life not in a community which was sunk in sloth, safety, and ease. There was no 'social security' in Athens, and no 'freedom from want and fear', for there was scarcely a moment in the history of its democracy when it did not stand in peril from without or within. It developed its greatest vitality when it was fighting for bare existence, and that which sustained it, until corrupting influences entered in, was Aristotle's 'energy of the spirit'. It is that quality which rings through the words of Pericles and has made them resound throughout the centuries. For here is a kind of existence which all intelligent men would wish to live —diversity; 'equality of opportunity' and respect for personal merit; tolerance, and freedom from the corroding poisons of envy and suspicion, law-abidingness, together with solicitude for the relief of the unfortunate and oppressed; sensitiveness to the influence of a healthy public opinion; beauty without extravagance, philosophy without the inertia of pure intellectualism; interest in public affairs and service to the State; free discussion of policy; training in citizenship by self culture; wealth for what it can give in real human values, but with no disdain for poverty, unless it be the result of indolence; relaxation of body and mind, taste and elegance and material well-being along with the pleasures of mind and imagination. All these things are to be found, expressed with perfection of language, in this imperishable utterance. Were they a romantic dream—rhetoric by Pericles and poetry by Thucydides? Did the little community of Athens ever really enjoy such an Elysian life as this? No doubt the colours were heightened, but there must also have been faithful portraiture in the picture, for otherwise this handful of men could not, in so brief a space, have erected such a monument in history and so deeply influenced the future of civilization. If there was reality in the picture. whal was the secret of it? I think we can find it in one immortal sentence of Pericles: 'because we deem that which is happy to be that which is free, and that which is free to be——' but how translate the Greek word εὔψυχον? Healthy-souled, high-minded, great-hearted, vigorous-spirited? It is impossible to translate Greek terms such as εὔψυχος, μεγαλόψυχος, καλός κἀγαθός—but I think we should all recognize the man to whom they apply if we met him in the Peiraeus or the Agora, and we recognize him if we meet him to-day—the man of magnanimous instinct, with a sense of the dignity of himself and others, free from the petty disproportions and ungenerous resentments which destroy dignity, and basing his uprightness in behaviour and conscientiousness in duty on the double obligation of respect for himself and consideration for others. It is such a man that the democratic way of life hopes to produce. It would be both arrogant and untrue to assume that no other system of government can produce him; but it is our belief that the democratic ideal gives more opportunity and scope for him than any other political system.

The two sides of his nature which constitute good citizenship are what Sir Ernest Barker calls his 'moral personality', the condition of which is liberty; and his sense of duty to the community, an obligation to make himself a well-developed part of a harmonious whole. It is essential that his sense of duty should arise out of his free-willing moral personality, and not out of a mere mechanical habit of blind, automatic, or superstitious acceptance of authority. Wordsworth has expressed it finely:

> Through no disturbance of my soul,
> Or strong compunction in me wrought,
> I supplicate for thy control;
> But in the quietness of thought:
> Me this unchartered freedom tires;
> I feel the weight of chance-desires:
> My hopes no more must change their name,
> I long for a repose that ever is the same.
>
> Yet not the less would I throughout
> Still act according to the voice
> Of my own wish; and feel past doubt
> That my submissiveness was choice:
> Not seeking in the school of pride
> For 'precepts over dignified',
> Denial and restraint I prize
> No farther than they breed a second Will more wise.

This duality of the individual self and the social self is individualism in the sense in which the present writer understands it and will, to the best of his ability, always champion it. The notion that the man who values, guards, and cultivates his own individuality is setting himself in opposition to the interest of society is a profound misunderstanding. It is the essence of democracy that the public interest cannot flourish without the cultivation of the individual's interest in himself. The Together-Will must be the aggregation of real and vigorous individual wills; otherwise it becomes that devouring monster, mass-emotion, goaded by unconscionable and overweening individual will. It is true that if excessive emphasis is laid on personal right the collective will is undermined and the general interest impaired. I have already suggested that the weakness of our democracy in the past generation has been to put too much stress upon personal right and claim. This is the real and cankerous egotism; and it is a strange paradox that those who to-day advocate the strengthening of personal liberty, initiative, and sense of responsibility are accused of encouraging mere selfishness, whereas it is precisely selfish interest which they seek to combat.

It is unquestionable that in the delicate balance between moral personality and civic responsibility, there is a constant danger that either the one or the other may be exaggerated. In the beginnings of American democracy, Tocqueville interpreted individualism (a term which he invented) as a new form of anti-social egoism, and he saw in it a menace to the future of democratic institutions. He wrote:

'Individualism is a novel expression, to which a novel idea has given birth. Our fathers were only acquainted with egotism. Egotism is a passionate and exaggerated love of self, which leads a man to connect everything with his own person, and to prefer himself to everything in the world. Individualism is a mature and calm feeling, which disposes each member of the community to sever himself from the mass of his fellow creatures; and to draw apart with his family and his friends; so that, after he has thus formed a little circle of his own, he willingly leaves society at large to itself. Egotism originates in blind instinct: individualism proceeds from erroneous judgement more than from depraved feelings; it originates as much in the deficiencies of the mind as in the perversity of the heart. Egotism blights the germ of all virtue: individualism, at first, only saps the virtues of public life; but, in the long run, it attacks and destroys all others, and is at length absorbed in downright egotism. Egotism is a vice as old as the world, which does not belong to one form of society more than another: individualism is of democratic origin, and it threatens to spread in the same ratio as the equality of conditions.'

Such were the fears of this acute observer for the future of American democracy. Have they been realized? I turn from these predictions to the latest book of American history known to me,[1] and I read:

'The core of the American, and of the English, philosophy of government is the individual. The individual is the source of government. He has rights and liberties in society; the right to worship as he will, to speak and to write, to go about his own business, choose his own work, marry whom he will, rear his family as he will, undisturbed by the State. No matter how socialized our thinking, our administration, our business has become, it is still true that the ultimate objective of our government and of our economy

---

[1] *America: the Story of a Free People*, by Allan Nevins and Henry Steele Commager.

is the creation and protection of the free man.'

These words are written by two distinguished Americans, of no reactionary tendency, about a society in which individualism has been seen at its worst and at its best—at its worst in the days of Reconstruction and the Carpet Baggers, of Frenzied Finance and of the Robber Barons, of the Pit and the Octopus, of Harding and Coolidge and Hoover and Normalcy, all periods in which rapacity and economic warfare were brought to a pitch which no theory of free competition could, in my opinion, justify; at its best in the indomitable hardihood and enterprise which opened up a continent and created a civilization in an incredibly short space of time. That spirit still endues the American nation with a vitality and a determination to overcome obstacles which we in this country have much cause to envy and which our common enemies have even greater cause to fear.

What are the prospects for the vigorous, self-developing, dutiful Democratic Man in our community of the future, and especially for the youth who will have to carry on the tradition of sane individualism, if democracy is to survive? There will not be new worlds for them to explore and to populate, no peak in Darien for a coign of vantage, but there will be an old world for them to cleanse and to fortify. Will they, so many as survive, be exhausted, petulant, and disillusioned, or will they have an 'energy of the spirit' to give themselves more of the 'full life' in order to be better citizens of their country and of the world? Will they come back with hands extended to grasp all the gauds and sweetmeats from the great Christmas Tree of the State, or will they extend their hands only to roll up their sleeves? Will the cry be 'Safety First' and

'Give me my due', or will it be 'Live dangerously' and 'Give me my task'—or at least, 'Give me my chance'? I do not know; but I do know that the future of British democracy depends upon which of these moods they will display. Legions of them, it would seem, especially those who have had the best of our education, are to be functionaries in Government departments and all their purlieus and by-ways, destined for the rest of their lives to be known in Whitehall and Pall Mall and the more respectable suburbs as what the French call M. Rond-de-Cuir. Mr. H. E. Dale (*The Higher Civil Service*) has described their life, their temperament, and their routine. It is a just and moderate picture, and it rightly repels many undeserved misrepresentations, but it is also a depressing picture. When one learns, for example, that the first few years of a Civil Servant's life—those very years which in other avocations are devoted to intensive learning, competing, growing, and emulating—are dedicated to crushing every particle of originality out of the individual and teaching him, above all, his own insignificance and his complete impotence to alter the settled ways, one does not see a breed of adventurous individuals and 'best brains' contributing greatly to the vitality of the nation.

The challenger which confronts democracy to-day is not a New Order; it is an Old Order coming back to earth. It is absolutism, which men accepted for so many centuries and which has suffered one comparatively short epoch of eclipse, remounting its throne. It is not Beelzebub going up and down seeking whom he may devour, but Lucifer, Son of the Morning, triving to regain his lost principality. In this present phase of history, may we not again see thesis and antithesis, and may we not hope for an ultimate synthesis? The acknowledged weaknesses and failures of democracy, its frustration of many of the high hopes which were entertained for it, have produced, by way of reaction, a return to absolutism, though in a new form. Will it come to pass that the antithesis will prevail for a long and bloody chapter in the history of man, or will the synthesis emerge in a chastened and purified democracy? On that issue hangs the fate of humanity, perhaps not only at this moment but for ages to come. What is certain, I repeat, is that this war will have been fought in vain unless a better democracy is born of it; and a better democracy will depend upon a better human individual.

INDEX

PRINTED IN GREAT BRITAIN
BY LATIMER, TREND AND CO. LTD.
PLYMOUTH